Nova Scotia's Historic Ferries

SHAPING NOVA SCOTIA

Nova Scotia's Historic Ferries

The Boats that Bridged the Province

Joan Dawson

NIMBUS PUBLISHING
NIMBUS.CA

Nimbus Publishing Limited
3660 Strawberry Hill Street, Halifax, NS, B3K 5A9
(902) 455-4286 nimbus.ca

Nimbus Publishing is based in Kjipuktuk, Mi'kma'ki, the traditional territory of the Mi'kmaq People.

Printed and bound in Canada
NB1752
Editor: Paula Sarson
Editor for the press: Angela Mombourquette
Cover: A postcard depicting the Halifax–Dartmouth ferry, ca. 1950s. [NS Archives]
Design: Jenn Embree

Library and Archives Canada Cataloguing in Publication

Title: Nova Scotia's historic ferries : the boats that bridged the province / Joan Dawson.
Names: Dawson, Joan, 1932- author
Description: Series statement: Shaping Nova Scotia
Identifiers: Canadiana (print) 20250217961 | Canadiana (ebook) 20250224836 | ISBN 9781774714737 (softcover) | ISBN 9781774714744 (EPUB)
Subjects: LCSH: Ferries—Nova Scotia—History. | LCSH: Ferries—Nova Scotia—History—Pictorial works. | LCSH: Ferry routes—Nova Scotia—History. | LCSH: Nova Scotia—History.
Classification: LCC HE5785.N69 D39 2025 | DDC 386/.609716—dc23

Canadä NOVA SCOTIA 

Nimbus Publishing acknowledges the financial support for its publishing activities from the Government of Canada, the Canada Council for the Arts, and from the Province of Nova Scotia. We are pleased to work in partnership with the Province of Nova Scotia to develop and promote our creative industries for the benefit of all Nova Scotians.

For Judy and Ray, who encouraged me to write this book

Contents

Preface

Ferries are part of my life, as they are for many Nova Scotians. In a province claiming more than thirteen thousand kilometres of coastline and known for its many coastal communities, ferries have played an integral role as people navigate the geography of the place they call home. I live in Halifax, where the harbour ferries form part of the municipal transit system, giving easy access to downtown Dartmouth and Woodside. When I have guests visiting from out of province, I make sure to take them on the ferry to Dartmouth and back, offering for the cost of a bus ticket a mini-cruise on North America's longest-running saltwater ferry service that affords as good a view of the two cities as a full-fledged harbour cruise.

In summer, I frequently use the LaHave River Ferry that runs between LaHave and East LaHave, situated in Nova Scotia's South Shore region. When I've travelled elsewhere in the province, ferries have transported me across bodies of water in places as far apart as Brier Island, off the western tip of Nova Scotia, and Englishtown, on Cape Breton's eastern coast and the site of French colonists' Fort Sainte-Anne in 1629. These provincially operated ferries are vital links in Nova Scotia's highway system, some providing the only access to communities, others shortening the journey by many kilometres. And today, we take them for granted.

The vessels that still operate are the few survivors from the days when ferries were the only means of crossing many bodies of water in what would become Nova Scotia. Most former ferries have been replaced by highway bridges or causeways. And, of course, ferry boats themselves have evolved over the years. Today's mechanically operated vessels, carrying both vehicles and passengers, bear little resemblance to their earliest predecessors, which were rowed by sturdy ferry operators across water that was often fast-running and turbulent. But they have all provided a valuable service to settlers and travellers and have become part of the fabric of Nova Scotia.

Until recently, fees were charged for all provincial ferries. The income they generated went toward their maintenance. This changed at the height of the COVID-19 pandemic, which was first declared in 2020. In order to maintain social distancing and protect both crew and passengers, intra-provincial ferry fees were suspended. When pandemic regulations were relaxed, and even today in 2025, travel on Nova Scotia's ferries remains free of charge.

Introduction

Nova Scotia is a peninsula—almost an island, except for the Chignecto Isthmus that forms a link with New Brunswick. Nova Scotia's terrain is scored by many rivers. For the Indigenous Peoples, primarily Mi'kmaq, who have lived here for thousands of years, since before European colonizers arrived on these shores, the rivers were not obstacles but rather highways that served the inhabitants' travel needs. Canoes, the regular form of transport for these early residents, carried them along and across rivers, lakes, and around the long coastline.

Early French settlers established their communities beside the water, which offered travel and trading routes in a time before roads were constructed. They ventured along the coast in trading vessels, and adopted the Indigenous means of traversing waterways by paddling canoes. Once communities of Acadians were established, the river crossings between them necessitated that someone would have a boat or canoe to offer; there was little need at first of formal ferries in most areas. Exceptionally, when British settlers came to Partridge Island, near today's town of Parrsboro, they found that Acadians had been operating a ferry service that linked their farming communities around the Minas Basin.

British colonists, too, settled by rivers and harbours. Between the existing geography and colonization, few of our towns and villages today are far from

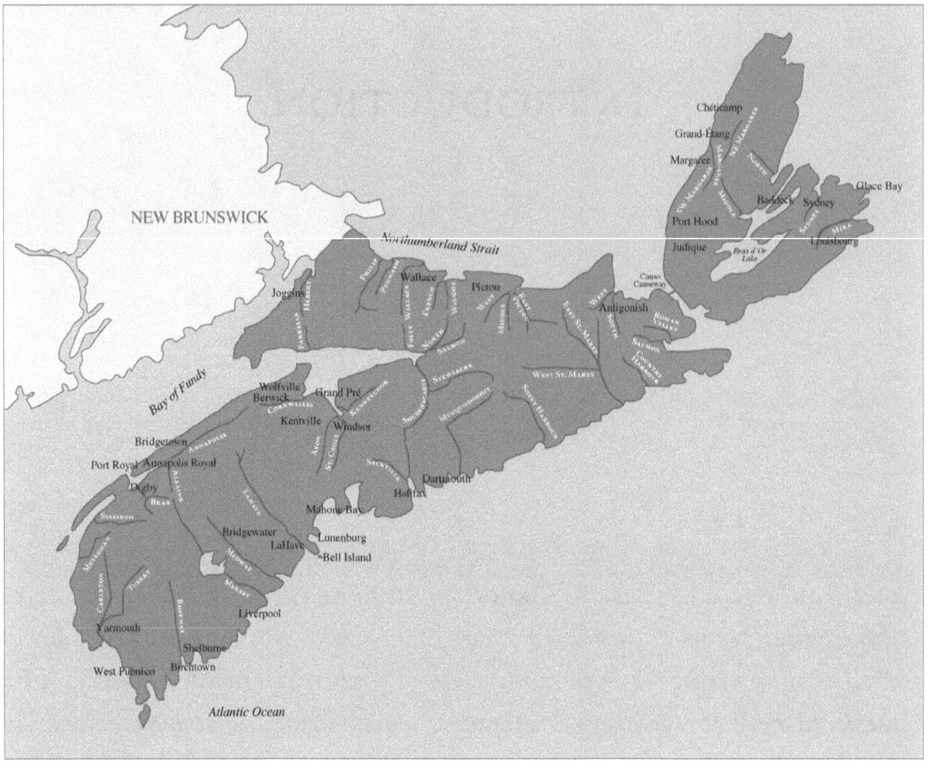

Nova Scotia's rivers.

a waterway. After the Expulsion of the Acadians between 1755 and 1764, the British invited Planters (which simply means settlers) from the New England colonies to take up the abandoned farms. The earliest Planter communities were small, consisting of only a handful of farming families. Their extended settlements might be scattered over some distance across a township, where a small town was laid out to serve as the administrative centre. The development of land routes between the settlements followed. The originally simple trails evolved into dirt roads. People began to travel between communities on foot, on horseback, or in some kind of wheeled vehicle—carriage, buggy, or wagon, and later, stagecoach.

As the population increased and travel between communities became more frequent, Nova Scotia's rivers posed major obstacles. Some rivers could be forded at low tide, and in some places wooden bridges were built. But a bridge was not a viable solution where a river widened too far. A traveller had to hire a willing boatman or make a detour to the nearest bridge, extending a slow journey. Inevitably, as travel increased, the demand grew for ferry services over these wider bodies of water.

Although most of Nova Scotia's ferries crossed rivers, in some areas harbours also caused problems. People often had to walk or ride a considerable distance around the head of a harbour to reach communities that were otherwise only a short jaunt away, across the water. If a harbour was not too wide, a ferry service was a welcome means to shorten the journey. Ferry service eventually linked islands, notably Cape Breton Island, to the mainland, and a number of other island ferries improved accessibility between settlements.

From the early nineteenth century, small communities scattered across the province were petitioning the authorities for financial assistance to establish and maintain ferries, and ready boatmen were requesting permission to operate them. The justices of the Inferior Courts and General Sessions of the Peace for the county in which boatmen lived issued the licences and set the fees. Usually these were in the range of a few pence (or cents, depending on how the official stipend was set) for foot passengers, more for cattle, horses, and carriages.

This system was confirmed by the 1873 Act for establishing and regulating Ferries. Once the service was initiated, ferry operators had to maintain suitable boats, with scows for vehicles and animals. Petitions from ferry operators for assistance with the maintenance and operation of their vessels became a regular part of the assembly's business. A sampling of petitions the assembly received in the mid-1800s gives evidence of the proliferation of ferries around the province in their heyday. Many ferry operators can be identified from their petitions for financial aid to repair or replace their vessels in order to maintain their service. Other ferry operators were named by residents petitioning on their behalf, but some remain anonymous.

In the 1920s, the fares were set at twenty-five cents per person, horse, or carriage, and per head of cattle; heavy team wagons cost fifty cents, while the few automobiles were charged two dollars. The act was most recently renewed in 1989, when the legislature reserved to itself the operation of the ferries at Grand and Little Narrows, Englishtown, Gabarus, Long and Brier Islands, LaHave, Tancook, Country Harbour, and Pictou Island. Nothing more was heard of a Gabarus ferry, but the others are still provincially operated.

Although ferries were public services from the beginning, in the nineteenth century there were far fewer travellers than there are today, so running a ferry was not a full-time job. There were no regular schedules; instead, ferry operators were expected to be ready to carry travellers across the water on demand. This commitment took them away from the farming or fishing by which they most commonly made their living, and they frequently complained that their revenues did not compensate for time lost. Many ferry operators depended on subsidies from the provincial House of Assembly to cover the expense of maintaining and operating a boat. Further challenges arose as some ferries operated seasonally. Some bodies of water froze and prevented the vessels from running in winter, while others were able to operate year-round. These were subjected to harsh conditions when they had to contend with ice, snow, and heavy winds, what was politely described as "inclement weather." The ferry operators' work could be dangerous, and their boats were often damaged.

In the 1850s, provinces became responsible for overseeing postal services, and Nova Scotia's legislative assembly required ferry operators to carry the mail free of charge. This obligation often meant extra crossings, occasionally at inconvenient times, with a scow for the postman's horse. Consequently, operators of ferries from Post Roads frequently asked for subsidies. As the population grew and the mail service was improved, the postmen needed to cross with increasing frequency, leading to further requests for financial assistance.

Residents and travellers were not always satisfied with the ferry operation. In theory, the ferry operator was expected to respond promptly to a signal requesting service. In practice, since most ferry operators were also fishers or farmers, if they were occupied there could be some delay in responding. The assembly received requests for additional funding to allow operators to ensure that they, or an employee, were available at all times.

Petitions to the assembly did not consistently feature only complaints. Archival records show that one ferry operator on the Minas Basin, for instance, was praised by residents for his good service, including his willingness to carry "Indians and poor people" free of charge. In this case the petitioners asked for a sufficient increase in funding to allow the operator to continue a regular service.

Ferries over rivers and harbours, across straits and out to islands, and eventually to neighbouring provinces continued for many years to serve the convenience of both residents and travellers. The ferry spared them many miles, and in some cases many hours, of travel to the nearest bridge or ford, or to the head of a harbour. Ferries were often operated in conjunction with an inn, or "house of entertainment," where travellers could obtain rest and refreshment.

Some of the nineteenth-century ferry routes that linked mainland residents to islands are still in service, but most of Nova Scotia's ferries have been replaced by bridges or causeways. Five of the remaining ones have become part of the provincial highway system; one, from the mainland to Caribou Island, is privately operated. Most have disappeared, leaving only a place name or street name to testify to their former existence, while others have vanished without a trace.

The original ferry boats were rowed, sometimes towing scows for carrying horses, cattle, sheep, or buggies. Over the years, rowboats were replaced by sailboats, steamboats, or motorboats. Today's remaining ferries are diesel operated. Almost all of today's provincially operated ferries carry trucks and cars as well as pedestrians. The exception is the Tancook ferry, which was originally scheduled to be relocated with a car-carrying service out of Blandford in 2024, but this plan has been delayed.

Two provincial ferries link Digby, Long Island, and Brier Island, crossing the narrow but turbulent Petit and Grand Passages between St. Marys Bay and the Bay of Fundy. In Cape Breton, short ferry runs carry vehicles and passengers from the mainland to Little Narrows, and across St. Anns Bay from Englishtown to the Cabot Trail. On the mainland, a longer ferry run crosses Country Harbour, carrying traffic between Isaacs Harbour and Port Bickerton. Perhaps the most scenic route is the LaHave Ferry's, with its view toward the estuary and the LaHave Islands. Since 2020, all the intraprovincial ferry services have been free of charge. They run to a schedule, but make extra crossings when traffic is heavy. Important ferries link Nova Scotia to neighbouring provinces: Prince Edward Island, New Brunswick, and the island of Newfoundland. There is also a ferry from Yarmouth, in southwestern Nova Scotia, to Bar Harbor, Maine in the US. Today, these are run by commercial transportation companies.

The memories of a few early ferries endure in place names or street names. Half a dozen Nova Scotian communities include the word "ferry" in their names, though not all of them maintain a ferry service. One exception is East Ferry, on Digby Neck, that is still home to the vessel that crosses Petit Passage to Tiverton on Long Island, while another from Caribou Ferry, near Pictou, has a privately operated service that runs to Pictou Island. Caribou is also the mainland terminus for the interprovincial ferry to Prince Edward Island. Granville Ferry is now joined to Annapolis Royal by a causeway, and the services at Grandique Ferry, Ingonish Ferry, and Jordan Ferry have long since been discontinued. In both Grandique Ferry and Ingonish Ferry, a Ferry Road leads toward the site of the former landing, but the ferry across Jordan Bay has vanished without a trace.

In this book we explore the history of many of Nova Scotia's former ferries, the people who operated them, and the communities they served. My research was concentrated on records in the Nova Scotia Archives from the mid-nineteenth century, when the majority of the province's ferries were operating. The few that remain operational remind us of the days when ferries were indispensable to travel in Nova Scotia.

The community of Ingonish Ferry, NS. [NS ARCHIVES, NEGATIVE NO. N-6401]

1
River Ferries

Nova Scotia's first ferries operated across rivers, which often separated communities that were only a short distance apart as the crow flies. In some cases, these ferries took the place of earlier fords, which travellers could cross on foot or on horseback. Although individuals might row across a river to the far side, as settlements grew so too did demand for more organized services. Petitions for ferries were sent to county officials, which led to the issuing of licences with regulations governing operation. Ferry operators were appointed to carry pedestrians, horses, cattle, and eventually wheeled vehicles across the rivers at controlled rates. The licence to operate provided protection for the ferry operator: it was illegal for any other person to carry paying passengers across the river. As roads were developed and travel increased, these ferries became a vital part of Nova Scotia's transportation system.

The ferry operations were often family affairs. The ferry operator usually ran a farm or other business; the ferry was a sideline, as traffic in early days of operation was sporadic, and the receipts from passengers were insufficient to make a living. Some operators ran an inn in conjunction with a ferry, offering their clients food and accommodation, to generate a modest income. A requirement of the operating licences was that ferry operators should be available at all times to serve the public. In other words, the licensee, either a family member or an employee, was expected to be continuously on call. A would-be passenger might request the ferry by waving a flag, blowing a horn, or beating a gong—and then wait for the ferry operator to arrive. The wait could be long.

Ferry boats needed maintenance, and although it was the county authorities that issued the licences and required the vessels be maintained in good working condition, it was to the provincial assembly that ferry operators looked to for subsidies. Among the financial losses that they claimed, in addition to the cost of necessary repairs, was the legal obligation to convey the postman with his horse and wagon free of charge, if they were operating on a Post Road. This often involved extra time and labour for the ferry operator or his assistants, causing frequent complaints.

Most of Nova Scotia's river ferries have long since been replaced by bridges or causeways. Only the LaHave Ferry survives and is now a provincially run service.

LAHAVE RIVER

Initially, the only way that residents of the communities on either side of the LaHave River could cross was by boat, until the construction of a bridge across the river in 1825 facilitated more traffic. Today's ferry running between

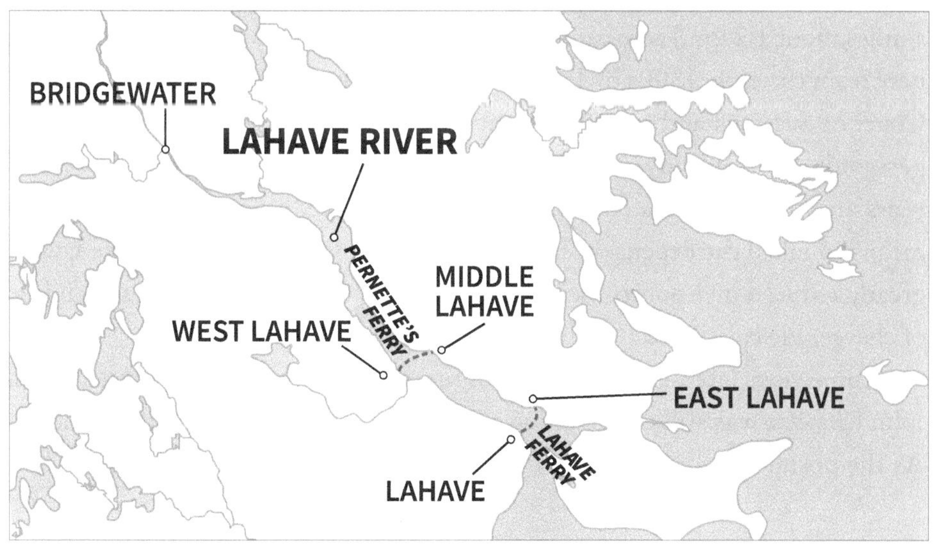

LaHave and East LaHave is the only survivor of a series of vessels that carried passengers and vehicles across the river over the years.

The LaHave River, or Pijinuiskaq (river of long joints), first served as a major travel route for the Mi'kmaq who lived along the river's banks, while they accessed the river for trading. The tidal portion of the river was first settled by Europeans in 1632, when the French built a fort at what is now LaHave. Residents of the fortified settlement crossed the river in their own vessels to tend the cattle pastured in the meadow known as la Vacherie on the east side.

Settlement on both sides of the river's tidal portion, between Bridgewater and the Atlantic Ocean, began after the founding of Lunenburg in 1753. Farm lots on the east side were granted to residents of the town. One of the residents, merchant Joseph Pernette, received a huge grant on the west side. It extended from the falls above Bridgewater to LaHave. Pernette brought in settlers to work on his farm, and a small community developed at West LaHave. There was also a small fishing population established at the river's mouth. In the nineteenth century, the population on both sides of the LaHave expanded. Residents made their living by fishing, farming, sawmilling, and boatbuilding.

The first LaHave ferry ran from a wharf below Pernette's homestead at West LaHave to connect with a road that Pernette had built from Lunenburg to today's Middle LaHave. At this point, the river was nearly three quarters of a mile (about 1.2 km.) across. A formally established ferry service was operated here from the early 1800s by Joseph's son John, who received a licence from the Court of Sessions and subsidies from the Legislative Assembly thereafter. In petitioning for a subsidy in 1830, he stated that he had kept the ferry for several years and though it was of great public convenience, his compensation by no means equalled the expense of labour and boats. His profits, he protested, were greatly reduced by a government order obliging him to carry the postman free of charge. He calculated this loss at five or six pounds per year.

Three years later, upon a request of funds for another boat to carry horses, John Pernette was still complaining about carrying the postman and his horse. As the postal system improved, Pernette continued to object: in 1834 he had to carry the postman once a week instead of once a fortnight, and by 1836 the postman had acquired a wagon and was crossing twice a week, even in "inclement seasons." The ferry had become an integral part of the postal system, regardless of how frequently those charged with the transporting complained. The road from the remains of Pernette's wharf on the west side is still known as the Post Road.

John Pernette was a farmer, a land surveyor, and an operator of a gristmill and sawmill on the brook that ran through his property. The ferry he ran, and the ferries others ran on the river, were necessarily seasonal; in the nineteenth century, there was ice on the LaHave River from December until spring.

When a bridge was built across the LaHave at Bridgewater in the early 1820s, traffic from Halifax to Liverpool and beyond was diverted from the ferry to the new bridge; however, for travellers from Lunenburg and residents on the lower part of the river, the ferry remained the most convenient way of crossing. George Wightman's map, made in about 1830, shows both the new bridge and Pernette's ferry, which John continued to operate until shortly before his death in 1852 at the age of eighty-four. His younger brother, Joseph, continued to run the ferry for some time, and it remained in the family. The community was for many years known as West LaHave Ferry.

By 1830, John's nephew, Charles Pernette, was operating a second ferry lower downstream. John was displeased because it diverted some of his traffic. Like many ferry operators, Charles also ran a tavern on the east side for the convenience of travellers. By 1856, his ferry was carrying the mail, and like his uncle, he was looking for further remuneration.

With the development of important fishing ports nearer the river mouth, another ferry was established in 1832 from Getson Cove, now known as LaHave. As the population increased and settlement spread along the river, in 1835 the Lunenburg County Court of Sessions approved a ferry run by the Wagner family, carrying passengers across the river to Millers Point at the village of Pentz. From Pentz, a road that is now only a rough trail ran inland to intersect with the Post Road to Liverpool and beyond.

Two ferry operators rowing a woman with her horse and buggy across the LaHave River, ca. 1900. [FORT POINT MUSEUM COLLECTION]

In 1884, ferries were operated by Joseph Himmelman from LaHave on the west side and by Peter Parks from Parks Creek on the east side. Local citizens petitioned in support of these ferries, seeking government grants equal to those accorded the Pernette ferry. Petitioners observed that the "said Ferrymen have more Labour to perform than the Middle LaHave Ferrymen owing to the river being free from Ice a longer period of the year every season than the Pernette Ferry and are now receiving less compensation." They requested an increase in the grant from thirty to fifty dollars each.

The Himmelman family continued to run the LaHave ferry for many years. In the 1930s, young Brady Himmelman often rowed the skiff across the river with his father, Andrew. Brady also worked on the family farm until leaving to serve in the Second World War. After the war, he returned to the ferry service

The Brady E. Himmelman, *a cable ferry that currently crosses the LaHave River from LaHave to East LaHave. Brady Himmelman was a long-time captain of the LaHave Ferry.* [DENNIS G. JARVIS, VIA WIKIMEDIA COMMONS]

in 1948 and served as captain for thirty-five years, while still overseeing the farm and additionally a Christmas tree lot. Brady Himmelman ran the ferry with a local crew until 1980, when the province took over the operation. He continued as an employee of the provincial government.

The equipment was periodically updated. By the 1950s, a scow with a ramp for motor vehicles was pulled by a motorboat, and by the time Brady retired a car-carrying cable ferry was running across the river. The latest cable ferry, the *Brady E. Himmelman*, is named after the man who had served on the ferry for so many years. It is now the only ferry across the LaHave River, sparing travellers a long drive up and down the river by way of Bridgewater. It carries fourteen cars and is used by residents and tourists alike.

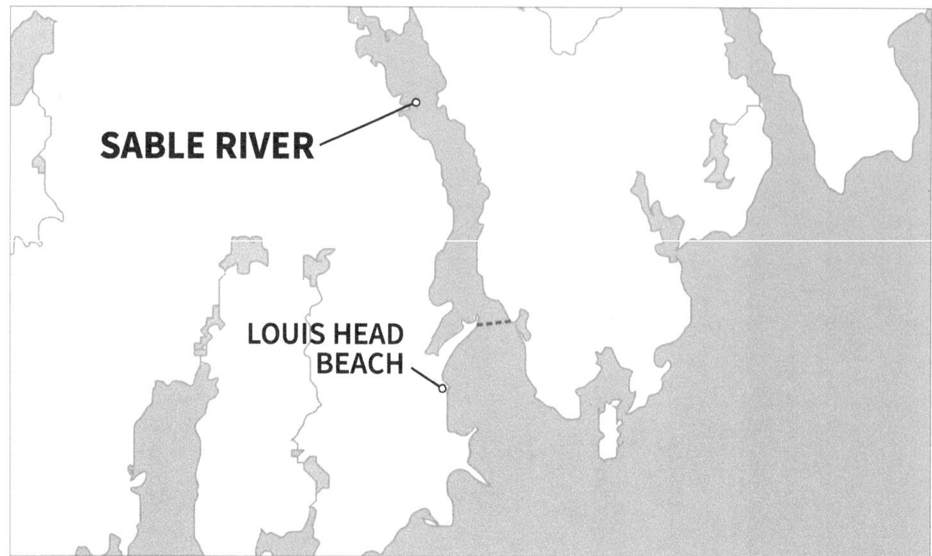

SABLE RIVER

Sable River, between Liverpool and Shelburne, was so named by early French explorers because of its sandy beaches. It has an extremely long estuary with a sandy bar known as Louis Head Beach that extends into the river, creating a narrow passage nine miles (fourteen kilometres) below the only bridge. The beach is now a popular destination for campers.

Although the population was sparse, those who lived along the lower river depended on a ferry to avoid a tedious nine-mile journey to the bridge at the head of tide. The ferry was operated by Cornelius Craig, who lived near a narrow spot in the channel created by the sandbar. By 1838, a now elderly Craig had found himself "compelled to ferry people over the river for little or no remuneration" for forty years. He applied to the assembly for "such relief as your Hon. Hous shall see fit." Like other petitions of this period, it was referred to the Committee on Navigation Securities. Craig continued to run the ferry for several more years, until at least 1844, repeating his request from time to time.

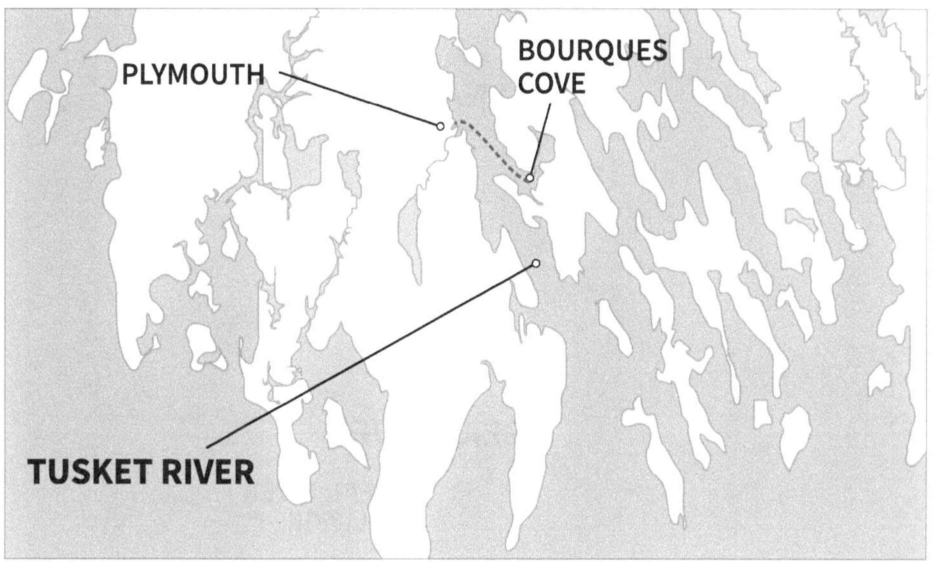

TUSKET RIVER

The Tusket River was known to the Mi'kmaq who lived in the area they named Nekataouksit (great forked tidal river). Acadians who had settled along the river in the 1700s were among those deported in the mid-eighteenth century. They had called the place Tousquet, which was anglicized to Tusket when it became home to Loyalists from New York and New Jersey in 1785. Shipbuilding became the basis of the economy, and the community prospered. Tusket was the main settlement in that part of Yarmouth County. The oldest surviving courthouse in Canada opened here in 1805. It now serves as a research centre housing the Tusket municipal archives.

A petition to the assembly in 1854 from the residents of Tusket Islands for support for ferries running between the islands includes a final leg across the Tusket River to Bourques Cove on the western side. It seems to have been successful: in 1855, a ferry described as being seven miles (eleven kilometres) below Tusket Bridge was operating and received a grant of six pounds from the assembly. The ferry between Bourques Cove and Plymouth was still running in 1912. Today, with improved roads, a bridge links Highway 103 across the river at the town of Tusket.

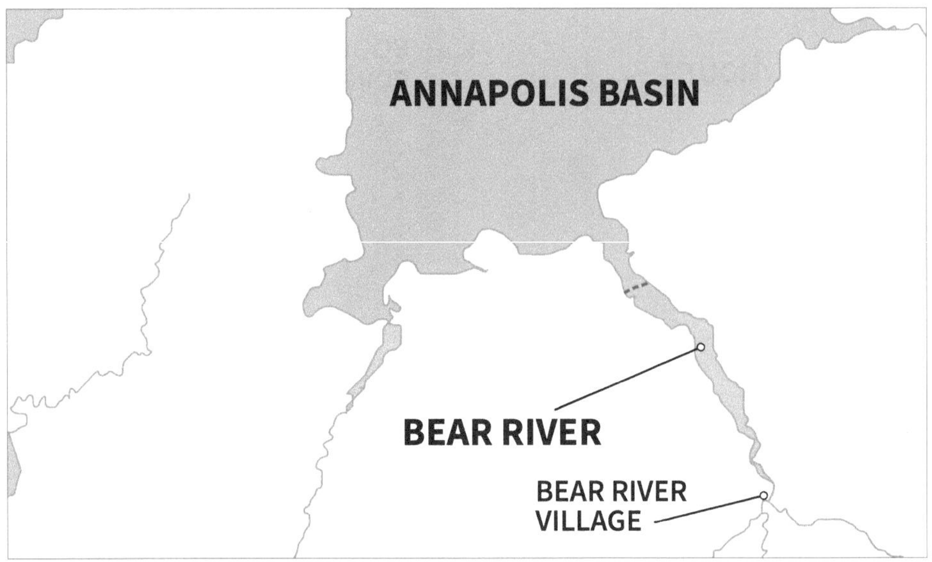

BEAR RIVER

Forming the boundary between Annapolis and Digby Counties, Bear River flows into the Annapolis Basin about eight miles (thirteen kilometres) east of Digby, across the basin from Digby Gut. The village of Bear River lies at the head of tide, where the two branches of the river come together, and the community spans both counties, as does Bear River First Nation. The Mi'kmaw community dates back thousands of years, and their name for the river is L'stitkuk (flowing between high rocks). The French, who founded Port-Royal in the early 1600s, named it the Rivière St. Antoine, and it subsequently became Rivière Imbert. Ultimately, the name was anglicized to Bear River. It is said that Louis Hébert, an apothecary from Port-Royal, planted the first grapevines on the slopes above the river.

In 1783, after the American Revolution, the British gave land east of the head of tide to disbanded German soldiers from the Waldeck Regiment, who had fought for them. English-speaking Loyalists formed the nucleus of the British settlement of Bear River, where they initially built log cabins at the head of tide. When sawmills were built in the area in the 1890s, the cabins were replaced by framed houses. Lumbering became the basis of the economy, and shipyards built sailing vessels that carried lumber to distant ports. Merchants imported goods from Europe and the West Indies. Because there was so little level ground in the settlement, many of Bear River's commercial buildings were constructed on stilts above the water. A bridge was built to connect the two halves of the community.

The Age of Sail ended at the closing of the nineteenth century, but the lumbering business continued; woodworking and barrel manufacturing remained important aspects of the economy. Wealthy vacationers enjoyed hunting and fishing with Mi'kmaw guides, and a tourist industry grew up in the twentieth century as visitors flocked to enjoy the area's beauty. In the later twentieth century, many artists and craftsmen were attracted to Bear River, supplanting the earlier businesses, and attracting tourists who also visit the vineyards on the slopes above the village. The people of the flourishing Bear River First Nation preserve their history in their Heritage and Cultural Centre with its Medicine Trail.

The Post Road, as it was designated at the time, from Windsor was established in the 1780s and initially ran only as far as Annapolis Royal, where the mail was carried by water to Digby. By the mid-nineteenth century, the road had been extended along the south side of the Annapolis Basin, but the wide estuary of Bear River created a major obstacle. In 1859, Charles Winchester had operated a ferry across the river mouth for a number of years. A petition to the assembly noted that this ferry carried only pedestrians, while horses and carriages had to travel over three miles (about five kilometres) from the Post Road to the bridge at the head of tide. The petition requested a grant of twenty-five pounds to provide a horse boat at the river's mouth. This seems to have been granted.

The ferry continued in service until 1900, when the one-lane Victoria Bridge was opened. Since 1972, the estuary has been spanned by a bridge carrying Highway 101.

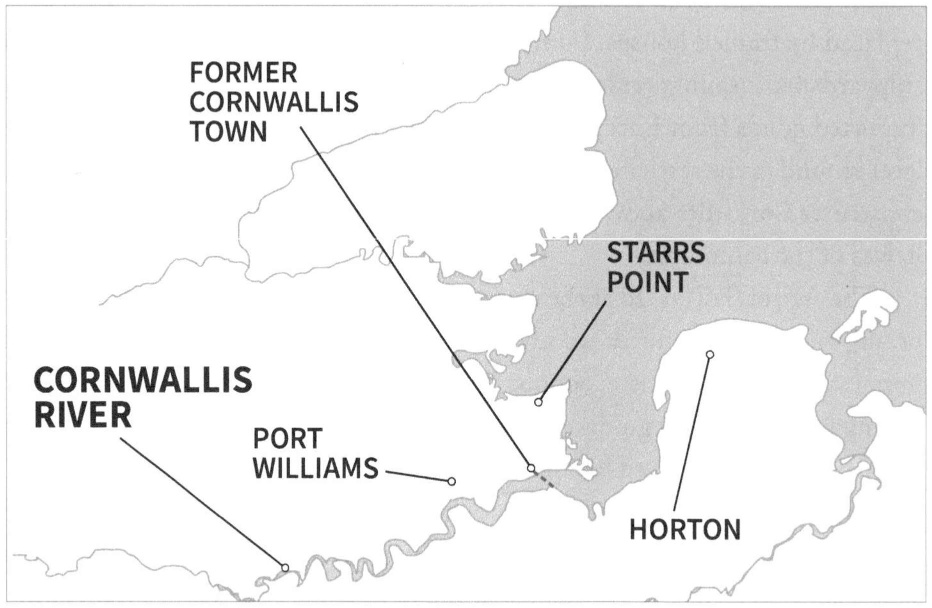

CORNWALLIS RIVER

From the early 1700s, the Acadian parish of St. Joseph des Mines lay between what is now the Cornwallis River and the Blomidon Peninsula. The river was then known variously as Rivière Saint-Antoine, Rivière des Habitants, or Rivière des Grands Habitants. Today's Starrs Point was known as Pointe-des-Boudreau, after the family who farmed it. The bank of the river, known as Côte-des-Boudreau, was the embarkation point for boats to and from other villages on the Minas Basin. The Boudreau family was deported by the British in 1755, along with the other Acadians from around the Minas Basin, and their farm, like those of their neighbours, lay abandoned.

In 1760, the Township of Cornwallis was laid out to receive a contingent of settlers known as Planters from New England colonies. The township lay on the north side of the Cornwallis River, formerly the Acadian parish of St. Joseph des Mines. The newcomers were granted the fertile farm lots that had not been worked since the Acadians had been deported. The town plot was laid out at the mouth of the Cornwallis River, at the site of the Boudreau farm, on what is now Starrs Point.

Cornwallis town was laid out in a grid pattern of twelve blocks with a central parade square. It was planned as the administrative centre for the township, with plots allocated for the usual civic amenities—church, school, and burial ground—and enough town lots for a considerable population. A ferry ran across the Cornwallis River from a wharf at the former Côte-des-Boudreau, to provide a link to the neighbouring township of Horton, south of the river. The pattern of the town's streets can be seen today, near Willowbank U-pick Farm.

The town plot's location on Starrs Point was very isolated, and without the ferry service residents would have to travel some distance upriver before coming to a crossing place. A bridge is thought to have been built at Port Williams in about 1780, but until then residents of the eastern part of Cornwallis Township were dependent on the ferry from the town wharf for access to Horton Township and the rest of Nova Scotia.

On the south bank of the river, a route across the marsh led from the ferry landing to the Post Road along the Annapolis Valley in what is now the Wolfville area. It seems always to have been poorly maintained. In 1774, the then ferry operator complained about its poor condition in a petition to the assembly. Known at one time as Ferry Lane, it has since vanished completely.

The Chipman family papers in the Nova Scotia Archives contain several documents that shed light on the history of the Cornwallis ferry and its operators. The first ferry operator was Caleb Wheaton, who subsequently moved away from Cornwallis. Before following him, his wife arranged for Moses Gore to run the ferry on an interim basis. Gore lived nearby and with help from his family was capable of maintaining the ferry. In an undated petition to "the Honorable Justices of the Inferior Courts and General Sessions of the Peace for the County of Kings County" Gore requested that the operation of the ferry be formally conceded to him. Perhaps rather in hope than expectation, he also "begs Leave to say that he thinks four pence for a Man and the Same for a horse is Full Little enough, Considering the Severrity of the weather a great part of the fall and Spring, and the Expence of Boats etc."

An increased fare seems to have been approved, but this did not sit well with the residents of Cornwallis. In 1769, the justices received a petition from the residents, protesting that the fare of "Six pence for man and one Shilling for man and horse" had been instituted because of the high cost at the time of "stock and provision with many other articles" and the expense of building a suitable boat for carrying horses and cattle and improving the track through the marsh. "Neither of which is done," they noted, "and as the price of the Articles aforementioned is much Lower, we are of Opinion, that four pence for man and Eight pence for man and horse is full enough."

The request for a reduction of charges was apparently granted as, in 1778, having operated the ferry for some time, Gore again petitioned the court for an increase in the fare. He stated that "Considering the Extraordinary Rise of prices of Provisions and other things" he found that operating the ferry had become "Rather a Burden than a profit." He asked that the fare, which had been fourpence per person or horse, be raised to "Sixpence for man or Horse or otherwise as you in Your Wisdom Shall think fit or best." A note inscribed on the cover of the petition states the raise to sixpence had been allowed.

In addition to operating the Cornwallis ferry, Gore ran a tavern, which was apparently not a very profitable business. In 1774, another petition from Gore stated that "as he is appointed to keep the ferry between...Horton and... Cornwallis, he is under a Necessity of Selling Spirituous Liquors and Victuals to Persons that pase and repase the said ferry, Especially in Severe weather, and the profits to be made thereby being so small he cannot afford to pay the Usual Sum demanded for License, by reason of the Number [of clients] being but few." He also wrote of the expense of employing several people to ensure that the ferry was available at all times, "Lest any person or persons Should be disappointed."

In the same document Gore requested that the road across the marsh on the Horton side should be repaired, "as it is now excessive bad both for man and horse." He further complained that some people were taking business from him by rowing people across free of charge, "or under a pretence thereof" perhaps being paid in kind or by an exchange of services. The practice took place mostly in summer, Gore acknowledged, leaving him the thankless task of rowing across the river in the coldest winter weather. A note at the bottom of this litany of grievances reads: "To be after Considered. Set aside." The result of the consideration is unknown.

Because of Cornwallis's isolated location, as time went on, most of the town's colonists moved away to their farm lots or to Port Williams and other communities. The bridge at Port Williams offered a permanent link with Horton Township and the Post Road. The ferry across the Cornwallis River became redundant and was discontinued.

ANNAPOLIS RIVER

The Annapolis River served as a major travel route for the Mi'kmaq and later the Acadians who built dikes and farmed along the river's fertile banks. In the late eighteenth century, the British government brought New Englanders, known as Planters, from the Thirteen Colonies to take over Acadian farms that had been forcibly abandoned in the Expulsion. Townships were surveyed and laid out on both sides of the river, each with a town that served as the centre

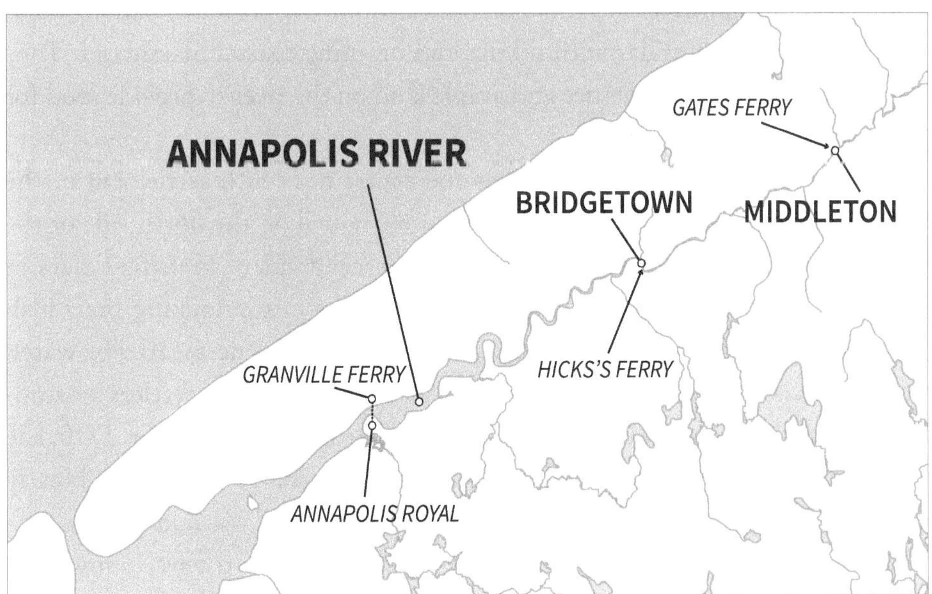

of administration. Over the years, communities grew up along the river, where residents were engaged in farming, lumbering, sawmilling, and shipbuilding.

Until the early twentieth century, when a causeway was built between Granville Ferry and Annapolis Royal, the Annapolis River was tidal as far inland as Bridgetown, where in early days there was a ford by which people could cross at low tide. Fords were also used on the river farther inland. As the population grew, ferries were established in place of the fords. Later the ferries in turn would be replaced by bridges.

GRANVILLE FERRY

The Annapolis River once flowed unobstructed into the Annapolis Basin, where the first permanent European settlement was struck in 1605. The Habitation at Port-Royal, built by Pierre Dugua de Monts on the north side of the basin, was made famous by Samuel de Champlain. Although the Habitation's structure was destroyed in 1613 by an English expedition, more French settlers were brought to Port-Royal by Charles de Menou d'Aulnay in 1636 to strengthen the settlement. D'Aulnay established the town on the point at the head of the Annapolis Basin, where the Annapolis and Lequille Rivers meet. Among these settlers were men familiar with diking and draining coastal marshland. They lost no time in creating pasture and arable land on the river to provide food for the residents.

In the mid-1600s, Port-Royal was the centre of French settlement in the area then known as Acadie. Land diked and drained on the north side of the Annapolis Basin was farmed by Acadians, descendants of French settlers in Acadie, whose small family villages lay on the slopes overlooking their lush farmland. Access to and from the town of Port-Royal was necessarily by water, but there is no record of a formal ferry service at that time. The settlers presumably rowed their own boats across. After the defeat of the French in 1710, the British took over Port-Royal and established a garrison at Fort Anne. Nearly sixty years later, after the Expulsion of the Acadians, land was laid out in townships on both sides of the Annapolis River and basin to receive immigrants from New England colonies.

Annapolis Township lay on the south side of the river. The former Port-Royal, now Annapolis Royal, had been the capital of Acadie from the 1630s and remained the capital of Nova Scotia until the founding of Halifax in 1749. In 1760, Annapolis Royal became the administrative centre for Annapolis Township. A significant military garrison remained at Fort Anne alongside the civilian population. The town became an important port, frequented by ships of the Royal Navy and merchant vessels.

Granville Township lay along the northern bank of the lower Annapolis River and Annapolis Basin, extending northward to the Fundy shore. The Granville town plot lay directly across the river from Annapolis Royal. The first grants were made to settlers in 1764, and the population expanded as new arrivals occupied the abandoned Acadian farms. By the nineteenth century, the population included farmers, merchants, and shipbuilders.

Water was the only means of transportation between Annapolis and Granville Townships, until a bridge was built in 1921. Naval and trading vessels had more important tasks than transporting civilians across the river. While some residents owned boats, a much-needed ferry service was established from Granville to Annapolis, which served throughout the nineteenth century and into the twentieth. It was operated around 1800 by Billy Johnson, the son of one of the officers at Fort Anne. An undated map that was made at approximately that time marks property owned by Johnson on the Granville side. Beside his name is the word "Ferry," and the settlement was for a short time known as Johnson's Ferry. Later it became Granville Ferry.

In about 1812, an inn called the Entertainment House was built across the street from the Granville Ferry slip to serve travellers using the ferry. By the 1830s, the brothers Harris and Lawrence Hall were operating both the inn and the ferry. The Halls also built an inn, near the ferry slip on the Annapolis Royal side, known as the Commercial House. Ambrose Church's late nineteenth-century map (page 26) shows the ferry slip on the Granville side and a matching one across the river with a hotel nearby.

The Entertainment House also served as a post office and livery stable for many years. For nine months in 1849 it was used by the Pony Express. This was

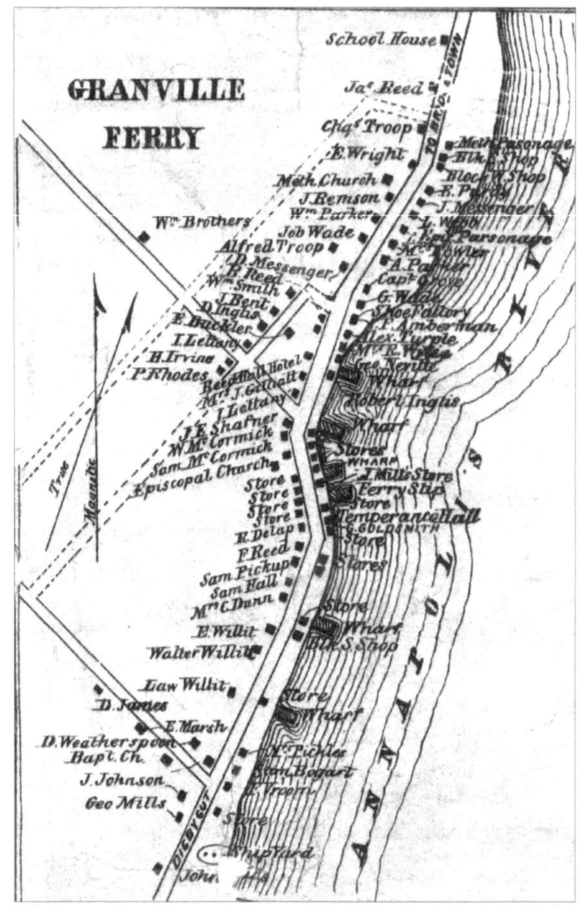

Ambrose Church's map from 1864 of the Granville Ferry area. The ferry slip can be seen at the centre of the map. [NS ARCHIVES MAP COLLECTION: F/239 - 1864]

financed by the Associated Press; horsemen carried packages of European news from a consortium of papers in Halifax to Victoria Beach on Digby Gut. From there, the news was shipped by steamer to Saint John, NB, where a telegraph station forwarded it to American east coast papers. The final change of horses on this lengthy trek took place at the Entertainment House at Granville Ferry. The service was discontinued when a telegraph station was established in Halifax.

The Granville ferry continued to operate for many years, but by the early 1900s the population on both sides of the river had grown, road travel was increasing, and the ferry was becoming inadequate for travellers' needs. Instead, a swing bridge was opened in 1921 to carry traffic across while still allowing vessels access to the Annapolis River. In 1961, the present-day causeway was constructed in place of the bridge, cutting off shipping on the river. Commercial shipping had already diminished as larger vessels came into use, and most freight was then carried by trucks. The ferry, long gone, is commemorated by the name Granville Ferry, the community on the north side of the Annapolis River.

HICKS'S FERRY

Farther inland, Bridgetown lies at the head of tide, at the site of the former Acadian settlement of Gaudetville in Granville Township. In 1765, John Hicks, a Quaker from Rhode Island, joined the British colonists in Granville Township. He moved across the Annapolis River in 1772 to land he had purchased in Annapolis Township. The population on the river's north side continued to flourish with the arrival of Loyalist refugees from the American Revolution.

In the early days of settlement, people crossed the river at a ford, but soon after Hicks's arrival he established a ferry for colonists' convenience, and the place became known for a while as Hicks's Ferry. Hicks died in 1790, but the ferry continued to operate into the early nineteenth century. In 1803, it was replaced by a wooden covered bridge, although for several years after the bridge was built the community name Hicks's Ferry persisted.

In the early nineteenth century, a prosperous shipbuilding business developed at the head of tide, attracting more settlers to the area. Captain John Crosskill, an entrepreneurial seaman from the West Indies with a checkered career, owned land at the centre of the community on the north side of the river. In 1821, he laid it out in an orderly grid, and the town's prosperous merchants and shipbuilders built many fine houses along the streets. In about 1824 residents chose the name Bridgetown.

In the course of the remaining century, the community prospered, shipping agricultural produce for export and developing a variety of small industries. Bridgetown was incorporated as a town in 1897. In the twentieth century, however, the development of larger vessels and the construction of the causeway across the mouth of the Annapolis River in 1961 ended Bridgetown's maritime activities. Today, a modern bridge carries traffic across the river.

GATES FERRY AT MIDDLETON

The Gates family were among a handful of settlers who came to Wilmot Township in the 1760s. They founded a small community on the Post Road that ran from Windsor to Annapolis Royal, halfway between the two towns, on the north bank of the Annapolis River. The settlement developed slowly at first, but the pace of growth increased in the 1780s with the arrival of Loyalists from the newly independent United States. The town lay at the intersection of the road along the Annapolis Valley and the road from the South Shore that followed the LaHave and Nictaux Rivers. To reach the intersection from the south, it was necessary to cross the Annapolis River.

The Gates family operated a ferry that carried travellers across the river, hence the early town name Gates Ferry. The ferry was an important factor in the development of the town, which grew up around the intersecting major roads. An inn established at the crossroads offered hospitality to travellers. In the nineteenth century, with the construction of a bridge replacing the ferry in the same location as the landing site, the name Gates Ferry became redundant. At a town meeting in 1854, the residents opted to rename the town Middleton because of its location halfway along the main road between Kentville and Annapolis.

The former alignment of Middleton's Bridge Street, according to long-time resident Gordon Rodgers, led from the main road to the ferry landing, which was a short distance from the present bridge. From the south side of the Annapolis River, the road to the South Shore joined today's Trunk 10. Mr. Rodgers remembers two old oak tree trunks on the riverbank, said to have been used to tie up the ferry boat at Gates Landing. Today's bridge and the alignment of the current Bridge Street have shifted slightly to the west.

THE AVON AND ST. CROIX RIVERS

The Mi'kmaq settlement called Pisiquid (junction of waters) lay at the confluence of the Avon and St. Croix Rivers, which these early inhabitants readily

Commercial Street in Middleton extended northward from the Post Road and the ferry. [ANNAPOLIS VALLEY MACDONALD MUSEUM]

navigated with birchbark canoes. The Acadians who came to the rivers around 1700 established a small settlement at Pisiquid. They drained the marshy lands along the Avon and St. Croix Rivers to create arable farmland. Family groups formed small villages, which were known by the names of these families.

On the upper Avon were farms worked by Germain Landry and his sons, Pierre and Germain, while the Foret and Breaux villages lay lower down the river, toward the Minas Basin on the Bay of Fundy. Although the two rivers separated Pisiquid from other communities on the Minas Basin, it was possible to ford the Avon at low tide, where a band of rock provided a firm footing. The ford provided access from Pisiquid to Grand Pré and the other farming villages around the basin.

On the west bank of the St. Croix River were the farms of the Hébert, Vincent, and Thibodeau families. (Descendants of the Thibodeau family still

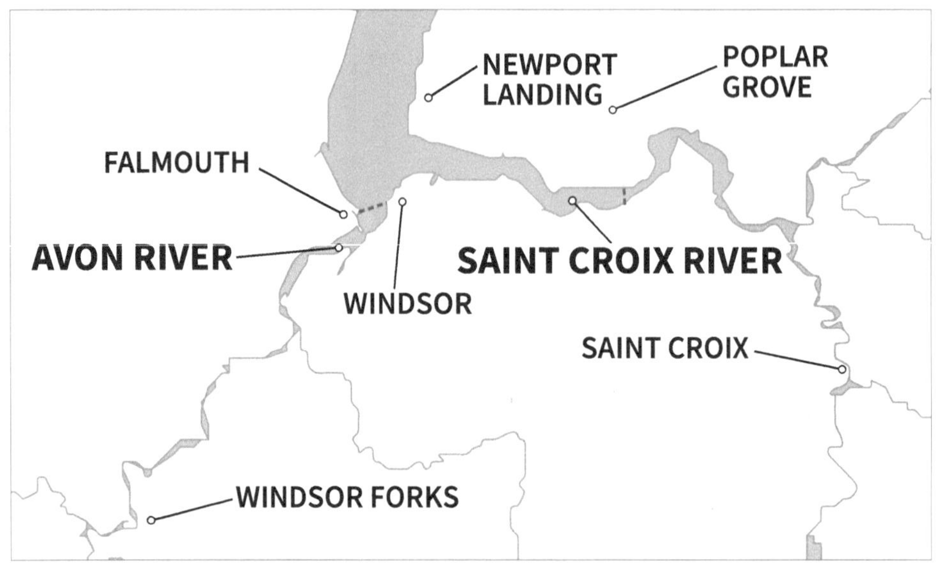

revisit their former farm every five years, at the time of the Congrès mondial acadien.) A ford just upstream from Wentworth Creek gave the Acadian farmers access to Pisiquid at low tide. There are no records of ferries at that time on either the Avon or St. Croix Rivers.

Soon after the founding of Halifax in 1749, the British established Fort Edward on a hill at Pisiquid, which they renamed Windsor. The fort overlooked the St. Croix River and the Avon estuary. As well as the troops in the garrison, some of the British settlers received grants nearby, and the small town of Windsor grew up at the foot of the hill. Initially, the residents used the ford to cross the St. Croix River. By the 1820s, the ford had been replaced by a ferry. Meanwhile, a bridge had been built farther upriver, at the village of St. Croix, to carry the "Great Road" from Halifax to Windsor.

In 1760, settlers from New England came to the newly created township of Falmouth, across the Avon from Windsor. The ford was available only at low tide, which was not always convenient. In the early 1760s, soon after arriving in Falmouth, James Wilson established a ferry from his riverside property to a landing below what became known as Ferry Hill. The service was taken over five years later by Jacob Brown. By the early 1800s, the ferry boat could carry a

John Elliott Woolford's King's College from the Ferry House, Falmouth *depicts a ferry crossing the Avon River.* [NS ARCHIVES]

horse. In the 1820s, ferry operator Constant Wilson applied for and received a grant of six pounds toward building a new boat or scow to carry horses.

Meanwhile, by 1800 another bridge had been built across the Avon between Martock and Upper Falmouth, where a direct road to Horton carried traffic from Halifax to the Post Road along the Annapolis River. But there was still no bridge at Windsor. The residents could either continue to use the ferry, or travel to the bridge at Upper Falmouth.

John Elliott Woolford's 1803 sketch *King's College from the Ferry House, Falmouth* shows the ferry crossing the Avon River with a passenger and a horse.

In 1816, Nathaniel Thomas Jr. and about sixty of his neighbours petitioned the legislative assembly for help to build a second bridge across the Avon, between Windsor and Falmouth town. The proposed site was below Ferry Hill, where the rocky riverbed that served as a ford could support the pilings for a bridge. The residents had already raised more than £1,100 toward the cost of construction but requested aid for the balance of the estimated cost of £8,000. It was not forthcoming, so inhabitants of Windsor continued to rely on the ferry.

In 1821, the assembly looked more favourably on the idea of a bridge, and authorized a lottery to raise the necessary funds. Work began the following year with the construction of an abutment; however, the lottery proved unsuccessful, halting the project. The ferry remained the only way to cross the lower river. A further attempt to obtain assistance in 1829, with a petition signed by residents of both Windsor and Falmouth, also failed, prolonging the ferry service. Finally, the private Avon Bridge Company was formed, approved by the assembly in 1834, and a covered toll bridge was opened in 1836. The ferry became redundant, but its name persists in what is still known as Ferry Hill.

In the early twentieth century, steamboats provided seasonal ferry services across the long, wide mouth of the Avon River, serving communities on both sides of the estuary. Originally operated by the Churchill family of Hantsport with their vessel the *Avon*, the service was taken over in 1910 by a group of Hants County residents with a new steamer, *Rotundus*. The ferry ran from April until late December, or until ice made conditions unsafe. The *Rotundus* operated daily out of Summerville, calling at Hantsport, Burlington, Avondale, and Windsor. The ferry's schedule depended on the time of high tide, when it could reach the wharves. As well as passengers and freight, *Rotundus* carried animals in crates. There were two cabins for men and women. The ferry operation ended in 1937, when a bus service was offered between the communities.

SHUBENACADIE RIVER

The Shubenacadie River runs about forty-five miles (seventy-two kilometres) across central Nova Scotia from Shubenacadie Grand Lake to the river's mouth at Maitland, on Cobequid Bay. The Mi'kmaq once paddled this major river in the sprawling area they call Sipekne'katik (where the groundnuts grow) from which the river's name is also derived. The territory extended over a wide area on the west side of the river.

SS Rotundus, *the ferry between Windsor, Hantsport, and Summerville, NS, ca. 1911.*
[NS ARCHIVES, B. R. ALEXANDER, 1984-497 NUMBER 213 NEGATIVE N-2829]

Acadian farms were established along the shores of Cobequid Bay and the Minas Basin in the 1700s. Small settlements grew up along both sides of the estuary of the Shubenacadie River, between Truro and Newport. On the river's west side, the village of Maitland in Douglas Township was once home to Jean Pitre and his family. In 1750, when conflict intensified between the French and the English for control of the land, the Pitre family moved to Île Saint-Jean (now Prince Edward Island). Following the Acadian Expulsion, confiscated Acadian property was redistributed, and the vacant Pitre land was granted to Halifax businessman Malachy Salter. When townships were established to receive Planters from New England colonies, this became the site of the administrative centre of Douglas Township. Originally known as Douglas, it was

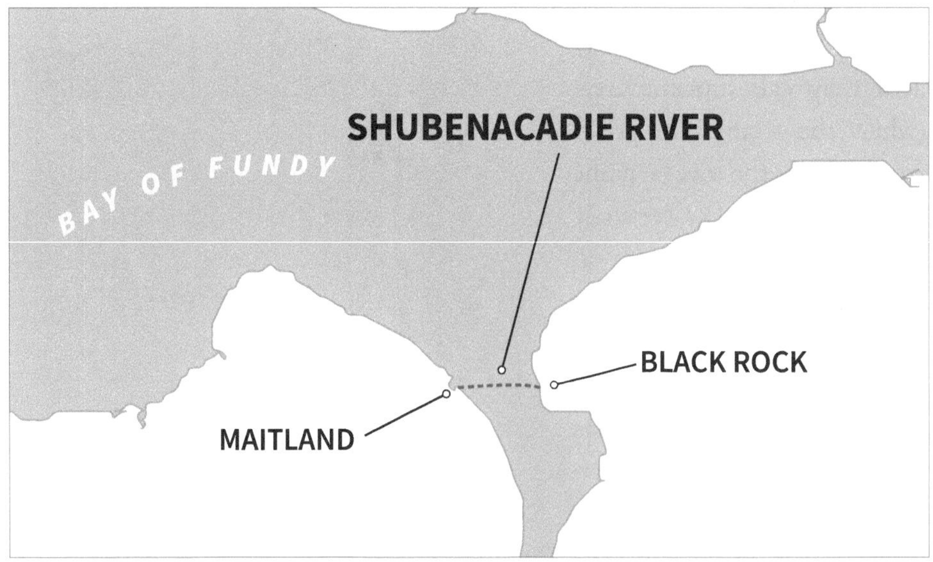

renamed Maitland in the 1830s in honour of General Sir Peregrine Maitland, who served as lieutenant-governor of Nova Scotia in 1828.

Salter did not develop his property, and it remained unoccupied until some families of Ulster Scots arrived in the area in the early 1770s. They revived the former Acadian farms, fished in Cobequid Bay, and in the early nineteenth century began to build ships, which became the basis of the community's economy. By the end of the century, Maitland had become a prosperous shipbuilding centre.

Maitland's most famous shipbuilder, William D. Lawrence, arrived there in 1855 and built himself a large family house overlooking Cobequid Bay. He established a new shipyard close to his home, where he built six ships. The last and most famous vessel, the *William D. Lawrence,* launched in 1874. Reputed to have been the largest wooden vessel built in Canada, Lawrence proceeded to sail around the world in it.

On the east side of the Shubenacadie estuary, a road from Truro ran parallel to the river's shore through the communities of Old Barns and Clifton, where Acadian farms had been taken over by settlers from New England colonies. Among them were Alexander Nelson and his family, whom we meet below.

The Shubenacadie, with its strong currents and wide tide range, presented a formidable obstacle to travellers from Truro to Maitland and those in the villages along the Noel Shore. Despite the estuary's turbulent waters, in the early nineteenth century a ferry service linked Black Rock, in Colchester County on the eastern side, to Maitland, on the west side. The ferry was operated over the years by different people. The road from Truro to Windsor came to the ferry landing at Black Rock, beyond the communities of Old Barns and Clifton. It was from here that boats left for Maitland and the road along the shore to Windsor.

A licence to run the ferry, and the regulations for its operation, were determined by the Colchester County Quarter Sessions in January 1819. The appointed ferry operator was Job Dart. In that same year, the assembly made a grant of twenty-five pounds toward the ferry's operation. By 1838, James Brown and Thomas Pearson were running a ferry from their inn on the Truro side. They petitioned the assembly for assistance, stating that the annual grant for the ferry had been withdrawn, and they hoped to have it renewed and to take over the ferry operation. Without the grant, they could not afford to maintain their boats.

Although their request was refused, the service seems to have continued. In 1839, the assembly received a further petition from Brown for assistance to maintain the essential service to Maitland, as the old boat was "perfectly useless and unsafe." The request was referred to the Committee on Navigation Securities. The immediate outcome is not known, but the following year James Brown and others were again seeking financing for a boat to carry horses, wagons, and luggage across the river to Maitland. They had received no aid, though the boat was unsafe and a danger to the public. Their request for twenty pounds was again referred to a committee. The wheels of government turn slowly, but in 1844, the legislature granted ten pounds each to "the two Licensed ferrymen at the mouth of the Shubenacadie...for the transportation of Horses and Carriages across that River." The ferry operator from the Maitland side is not named.

By 1852, John Copeland was running a ferry between Black Rock and Maitland and receiving an annual grant of ten pounds toward the ferry's operation. He now considered this sum inadequate because of the recently passed legislation obliging ferry operators to transport the mail. This meant that he had to convey the postman and his horse across the river free of charge, which necessitated extra crossings. Copeland petitioned the assembly for additional funds to cover this expense. In 1857, either Job Dart or his son was running two boats across the river, one capable of carrying a horse and carriage. In this year, Dart appealed to the assembly for financial assistance to replace the vessel.

In 1854, Isaiah Smith appealed for fifteen pounds to build a ferry boat from Douglas to the Truro road. A Mrs. Smith, probably his wife, seems to have been left in charge of the ferry. We do not know who she employed to operate it.

The ferry system seems to have stabilized later in the century. The Nelson family had been established in the Old Barns area near the Shubenacadie River since 1761, when Alexander Nelson, a Scot who had immigrated to Boston, received a grant in Old Barns after serving under General James Wolfe at Quebec. Alex's son Elias, born in 1783, assumed the operation of the ferry running from Black Rock early in the nineteenth century. He continued the service for fifty years. According to an article in the *Truro Daily News*, members of the Nelson family ran the Black Rock ferry for over one hundred years.

The 1873 Act for establishing and regulating Ferries set the fees. In the early 1920s, the standard charge for a person, horse, or carriage was twenty-five cents; a heavy wagon cost fifty cents, and cattle twenty-five cents per head. Cars were charged two dollars.

In the twentieth century, the ferries became mechanized. The Nelsons' last three ferry boats were *Liberty Hall*, a sailboat with an engine, launched in 1899; replaced by *Ethel May*, also equipped with a sail and a marine engine, in 1912; and *Eunice*, brought into service in 1921. The last two could carry several horses and carriages, or cars. *Eunice* offered a roll-on, roll-off service for six cars.

In 1817, the Shubenacadie River was bridged at South Maitland, where the present road bridge links Trunk 236 across the river. The ferry service across the Shubenacadie continued until 1934, when it was discontinued.

PUGWASH RIVER

Cumberland County's community of Pugwash lies on the east side of the estuary of the eponymous river, which comes from the Mi'kmaw name Pasgwesk, referring to a shoal near the harbour mouth. Indigenous population of the area began soon after the retreat of the ice sheet from Nova Scotia, about 13,500 years ago. Acadians lived there from the 1660s until the Expulsion, followed by Loyalist settlers in the 1790s. At that time, the town was laid out in an orderly, gridiron fashion, on the east side of where the Pugwash River flows into the Pugwash Harbour. The river runs through a low coastal plain, widening just before it reaches the coast, where it suddenly narrows again.

The site was formally purchased from the Mi'kmaq by the Seaman family in 1802. Gaelic-speaking Scots immigrants crossed the Atlantic from the Highlands in the nineteenth century, and Gaelic was spoken in the community for many years. Street signs in Pugwash are bilingual, a nod to the village's Scottish heritage.

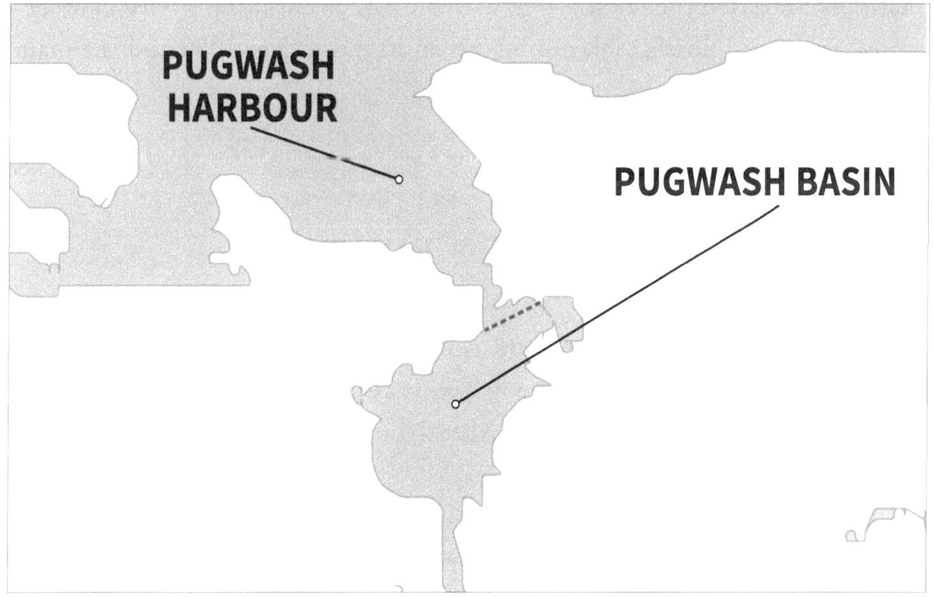

For some time, the settler population, consisting mainly of fishers, would use their own boats to cross the narrow channel to reach the west side of the river and the road to Amherst. They may have taken their neighbours on occasion. By the 1840s, a more regular ferry was needed, and the Court of Sessions appointed Maurice Walsh as ferry operator. At considerable expense Walsh purchased boats—presumably a rowboat and a scow—for horses and carriages as well as foot passengers. In 1844, he asked the assembly for help, because "owing to the great shortage of money in the county" the revenue from his passengers did not cover his expenditures. He needed assistance to continue operating the ferry. Like other requests at this time, it was forwarded to the Committee on Navigation Securities.

Later in the century, the ferry was operated by Donald McKinnon and three appointed ferry operators. The vessel carried foot passengers, horses, and wagons. It had also carried the mail to Amherst free of charge twice a week until the government agreed to pay McKinnon five pounds. A ferry continued to cross the narrow river mouth until a bridge was built.

The Intercolonial Railway came to Pugwash in the 1870s, bringing visitors to the community. A disastrous fire in 1898—one of four major fires that dramatically impacted the village—destroyed many houses, along with churches, stores, mills, and hotels. Salt mining began in the area in 1959 and is a mainstay of the economy today.

SYDNEY RIVER

The Sydney River runs into the south arm of the harbour at the town of Sydney, which lies on the east side. Before a bridge was built, a ferry ran across the river from the town of Sydney River to Coxheath on the opposite bank and the road leading westward.

For some years before 1855, Neil McLellan had been running the ferry with no government support, but he now requested "a small sum" to maintain

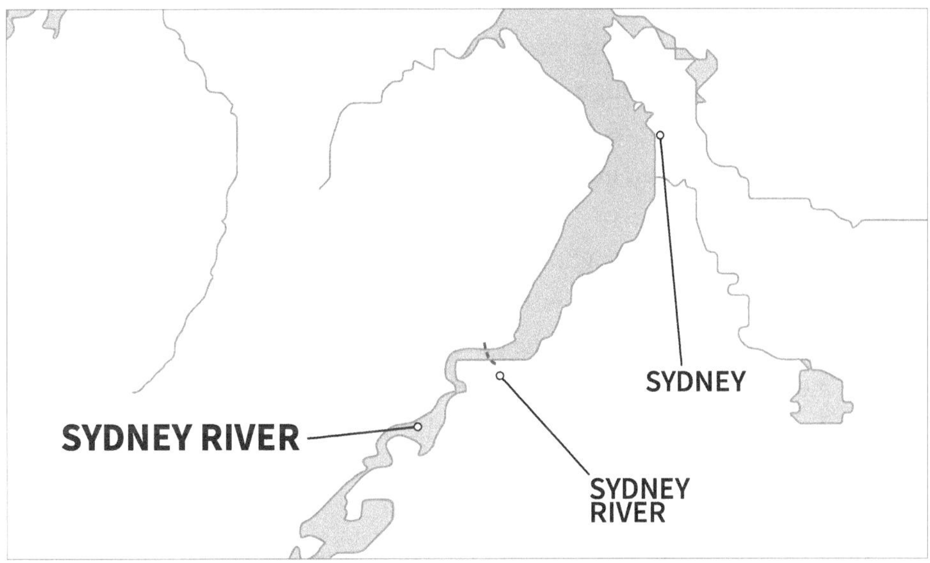

the service, which he threatened would otherwise discontinue. He seems to have been successful, as by 1866 there were ferry operators on each side of the river who were receiving an annual grant of ten dollars each. This they considered inadequate; they claimed that servicing and running the boats was a full-time job, and the meagre income they received from their passengers did not cover their expenses. They petitioned the assembly for an increase to twenty dollars for each ferry operator, and they, too, threatened to withdraw their services unless this was granted. Their Member of Parliament supported the request, but the outcome was not recorded. It is likely that the service continued, though the terms are not known, until a land bridge was constructed.

THE MIRA RIVER

Travellers between Sydney and Louisbourg may have noticed a store bearing the name Mira Ferry Market that is attached to a gas station at Albert Bridge.

Where, they may ask, is the ferry? Today, the community of Albert Bridge takes its name from the highway bridge across the Mira River that was first known to the Mi'kmaq as Sookakade (the silver place). In earlier days, the crossing would have been made by boat, and its memory is perpetuated in the store's name.

In the first half of the eighteenth century, the Fortress of Louisbourg was the principal community in the French colony of Île-Royale. Its inhabitants included the military garrison, the governor and administrative officers, merchants, monks and nuns, fishers, and tradesmen. Much of their food supply had to be imported, but a fertile area on the banks of the river, then known as the Miré, supported farms whose fresh produce supplemented the vegetables grown in the residents' gardens.

Some of these farms were operated by soldiers from the garrison, others by civilians. A large farm on the south side of the Mira was worked on behalf of the Brothers of Charity to provide fresh food for the brothers who ran a hospital in the fortress and for their patients. On the north side, where the river narrows, a productive farm was operated by Mathurin Le Faucheux, who received a concession there in 1734. His farm was linked by boat to his neighbours on the south side and to the fortress.

After the final fall of Louisbourg, the control of Île-Royale passed to the British, who changed its name to Cape Breton Island, although they did not begin to bring settlers until after 1784, when land was granted to accommodate an influx of Loyalists. Most of these newcomers settled in Sydney, but there was also a small fishing population in Louisbourg. A small group of Gaelic Scots took over the farmland formerly worked by the French on what was now known as the Miray, or Mira River. The community lay on the route from Sydney to Louisbourg, and by 1794 an official ferry had been established there, marked on a map of that date as the King's Ferry.

The ferry operated for many years, and the community became known as Mira Ferry. The name persisted for some time after a bridge was built across the river in 1849 to accommodate the increase in traffic. This was also the year

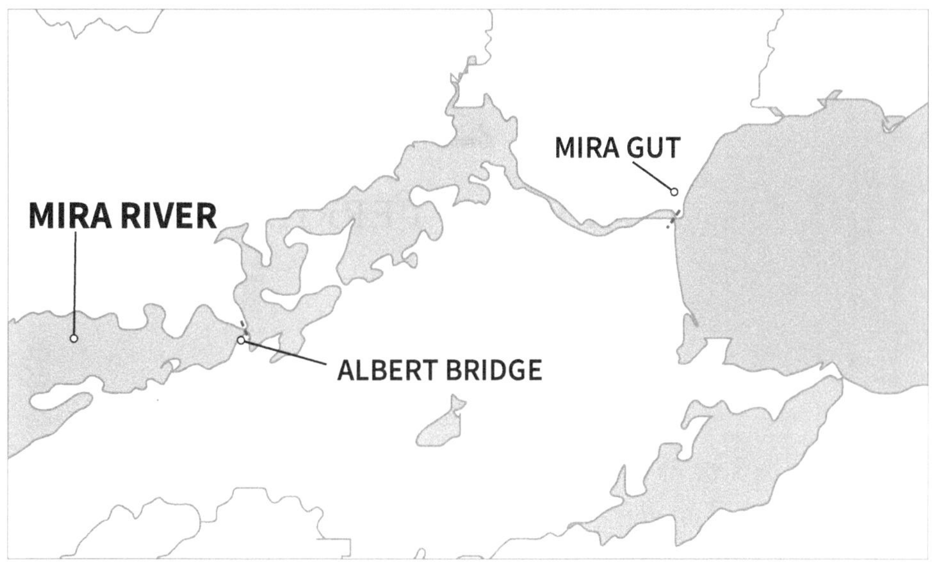

that construction began on the Union Presbyterian Church on the south side of the river, overlooking the ferry crossing. The bridge was well established by the time the church opened in 1857; however, it was still known as the Ferry Church for many years after the official name of the community had become Albert Bridge. The bridge was possibly named not for the prince consort but for Albert Munro, whose father served in the British parliament and had been instrumental in getting the bridge built. It was replaced in the 1970s with the present-day bridge.

A different form of ferry service was provided for some years, with steamboats criss-crossing the river from Mira Gut to Victoria Bridge. The first steamer, known as the SS *Barleycorn*, was twenty-five feet (eight metres) long and went into service in about 1895. Larger vessels came into use in the twentieth century, usually with two running at the same time. The boats called at the communities on each side of the river like a local bus service until 1926, when passenger traffic had dwindled with better roads and the increasing use of cars. Ultimately, the service ceased.

2
Harbour Ferries

Many of Nova Scotia's harbours are narrow inlets on the shoreline, while others lie at the head of wide bays. Until recently, most of them were busy with fishing and trading vessels steadily coming and going. Communities of farmers and fishers developed along the shores of many of the province's harbours. Those who lived near a harbour's entrance in the early nineteenth century could perhaps see their neighbours on the far side, but in order to meet, they had to travel to the head of the harbour. Similarly, a road along the shore created a diversion, which in some places added a considerable distance to a journey. But by the mid-nineteenth century, ferries crossing some of Nova Scotia's harbours provided more expedient access to the far side for residents and travellers alike.

Following the establishment of the Halifax Harbour ferries, which have run constantly since shortly after the founding of the city, more ferries appeared on other Nova Scotian harbours. Even after motorized vehicles shortened the time needed to drive around a harbour, in some places people have still been glad to have the services of a ferry operator. As with the river ferries, county courts issued licences to the harbour ferry operators, and subsequent funding came from the legislative assembly.

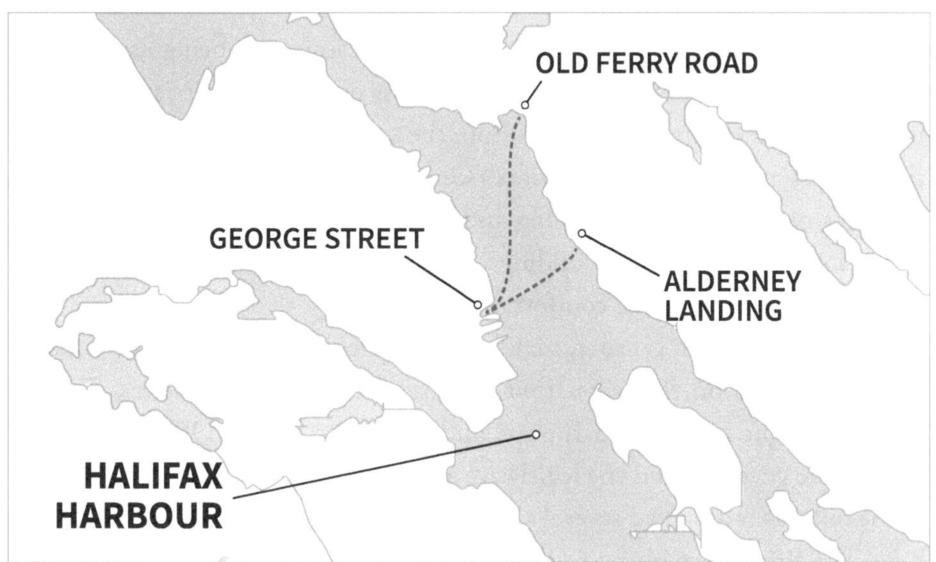

HALIFAX HARBOUR

When Halifax was established as the capital of Nova Scotia in 1749, a site was selected on the northern shore of what was then Chebucto Harbour. "Chebucto" is the anglicization of the Mi'kmaw name Kjipuktuk (great harbour). The site of colonially named Halifax held sacred significance to the Mi'kmaq, but the settlers, indifferent to Indigenous Peoples' cultures, proceeded to build their new town in spite of protest. Ships brought British settlers, who built rough cabins for quick shelter until they were established. Expanding the population were Boston businessmen, who saw opportunities for profit in the new capital.

Halifax was laid out in a grid form, seven blocks deep and five blocks wide, surrounded by a palisade with five forts. A parade ground was set out in the town's centre, with provision for a church at one end and a courthouse and prison at the other. The governor's house stood nearby, one block from the harbour.

Most newcomers initially lived in simple log cabins, but the better-off citizens aspired to framed houses, constructed with lumber that was supplied from a sawmill also set up in 1749 across the harbour, in what is now Dartmouth.

In spite of resistance by the Mi'kmaq whose territory was being usurped, the sawmill continued to operate and was the first of many industries that would flourish in that community. Wood from the sawmill was used in the construction of St. Paul's Church on Halifax's Grand Parade. Completed in 1750, it is the city's oldest surviving building and still serves its Anglican congregation. Work also began on official buildings, and prosperous residents started to construct what would become comfortable homes.

In the nineteenth century, Halifax grew quickly. Merchants built wharves and warehouses on the waterfront and fine homes for themselves. Trading vessels brought goods from Europe and the West Indies. Official buildings housed the governor and the legislative assembly, and the small fort at the top of the hill was redesigned several times to become the Citadel, a major military base. The British established a dockyard north of the town, which served for half the year as the main North Atlantic station for the Royal Navy. Soldiers and sailors swarmed the town's streets, and brothels and taverns thrived.

Across the harbour, settlement also expanded. In 1750, the ship *Alderney* had brought settlers from Britain to the east side of the harbour, again without regard for the existing Mi'kmaw hunting and fishing grounds. The settlement established there, named Dartmouth, was laid out in the same orderly fashion as its counterpart across the harbour. Augmenting the settlers from the *Alderney*, Loyalists arrived after the American Revolution. Scottish and Irish immigrants made their homes there as well. The original Mi'kmaw settlement was reduced to a small area known as Turtle Grove. Industries sprang up, powered by the brook from Albro Lake. For a while after the American Revolution, during which many Quaker ships were lost, Quaker whalers came from New England, built homes, docked their vessels, and processed their catch in the town.

Many people were brought to the area in the nineteenth century to build the Shubenacadie Canal. The project was a massive undertaking of ultimately more than sixty miles (one hundred kilometres) of waterway that included locks. Vessels were carried from the harbour by way of a hydraulic lift to the lakes behind Dartmouth, and through Shubenacadie Grand Lake to the

Shubenacadie River. Construction was completed in 1861. Ten years later, the canal was closed, giving way to a railway that crossed the province.

Soon after the founding of Halifax and Dartmouth, boats criss-crossed the harbour bringing lumber from the sawmill on the Dartmouth side, and transporting people back and forth between communities. In 1752, a formal ferry service was introduced, which has the distinction of being the oldest saltwater ferry service in North America. By order-in-council, John Connor was issued with a charter to operate this ferry. There was no fixed schedule; during daylight hours on weekdays, if a passenger appeared on the wharf, Connor rowed his boat across the harbour. The fare was threepence. Connors's appointment was for three years, but after running the ferry for only one year, he relinquished the business, which changed hands twice more before 1786.

In about 1797, soon after coming to Halifax, John Skerry established a new ferry service between Dartmouth and Halifax. It consisted of two large scows, each powered by two oarsmen, which carried passengers, freight, and livestock across the harbour. By 1815, a second ferry, the Lower Ferry (as it was known), ran from farther south on the Dartmouth side. It was owned by James Creighton and leased to Joseph Findlay. Both ferries landed at the Market Slip in Halifax, at the foot of George Street, close to the present ferry terminal. In 1816, a mechanized ferry named the *Sherbrooke* was introduced for the harbour crossing. Known as the team boat, it was operated by eight or nine horses that walked in a circle on the deck, powering a cogwheel that turned a central paddle.

The team boat was replaced in 1830 by a steam-powered ship, *Sir Charles Ogle*. This was a side-paddled vessel built in Nova Scotia and operated by the Steam Boat Company. The company's other boats, also steam-powered, included the *Chebucto* and the *Micmac*. From 1890 to 1909, the Dartmouth Ferry Commission operated the *Halifax*, a double-ended, side-paddled ferry.

The commission ran a series of ferries in the twentieth century that carried cars as well as passengers. In 1944, a fire broke out on the *Governor Cornwallis*, which had been in service for only two years and was subject to mechanical problems. The crew controlled the fire until the vessel docked and

The Sir Charles Ogle, *which operated from 1830 to 1894, was the first steam ferry-boat between Halifax and Dartmouth.* [DARTMOUTH HERITAGE MUSEUM]

Fire broke out on The Halifax–Dartmouth ferry the Governor Cornwallis *on December 22, 1944.* [DARTMOUTH HERITAGE MUSEUM]

A modern Halifax–Dartmouth ferry, the Viola Desmond. [COLIN STEPNEY VIA WIKIMEDIA COMMONS]

the passengers were safely ashore, but the *Cornwallis* could not be saved. The vessel was towed to Georges Island, where it burned on the beach.

There were fewer vehicles on the ferries once the Angus L. Macdonald Bridge was opened in 1955. The car-carrying vessels were soon replaced by ferries carrying only passengers. The service was taken over by the Metropolitan Authority in 1994, and it became part of the Halifax Regional Municipality's transit system.

Halifax Harbour today is spanned by two bridges across The Narrows. It is also served by diesel-powered ferry boats on two routes from downtown Halifax: one to Alderney Landing in downtown Dartmouth, and one to Woodside, farther southeast down the harbour. These ferries are the latest in a long series of vessels that have served the citizens of Halifax and Dartmouth and travellers from beyond since the mid-eighteenth century. With seats in the cabin and on the upper deck, for the price of a bus ticket they offer spectacular views of both sides of the harbour that residents and tourists alike enjoy. A third ferry service is now planned, using electric-powered vessels to run from several points on the Bedford Basin to downtown Halifax.

NORTHWEST ARM

Known to the Mi'kmaq as We'kwaltijk (end of the bay), the Northwest Arm on the western side of Halifax Harbour is approximately 2 miles (3.5 kilometres) long and 0.3 miles (0.5 kilometres) wide. The narrow channel, widely known as the Arm, has been home to small fishing villages, industries, residential communities, grand estates, yacht clubs, parks, and two prisons, all of which contributed to the need for public transportation from one side of the inlet to the other.

In the 1750s, soon after the founding of Halifax, a sawmill was constructed on the brook that falls into the Northwest Arm from what is now Chocolate Lake. In the nineteenth century, the brook became the site of various industries, including a gristmill, a snuff mill, a foundry, and the chocolate factory from which the lake takes its name. Farther south along the Arm's shore, Williams Brook, running down from Williams Lake, originally powered a gristmill, followed by other milled products. Quarries on the western side of the Arm were the source of building materials for Halifax. Today, the quarry area below Williams Lake houses the Royal Nova Scotia Yacht Squadron and the Saraguay Club. Along with early industries, there were small fisheries on the far side of the Arm, set up with their wharves and fish sheds. Residential communities became established that were home to workers in the fisheries and other industries. Today, the industries have gone, but the communities remain.

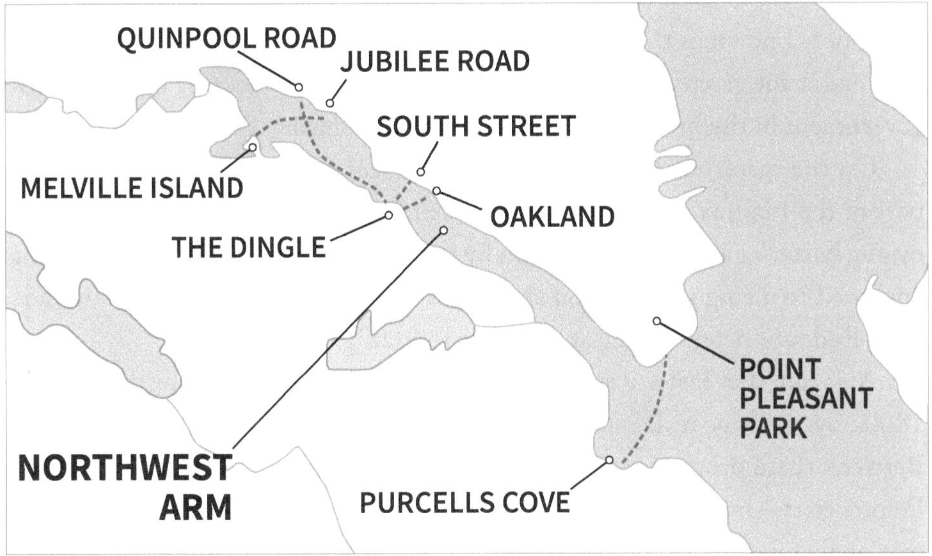

There are two small peninsulas in the Northwest Arm that are named as islands and that bear their own history. Melville Island, on the western side of the Arm, was selected during the Napoleonic Wars as the site of a prison, and from 1803 French captives were held there. The War of 1812 brought American prisoners to the island. Subsequently, the prison building was used to house Black American refugees who had escaped on British ships near the end of the war. Next, it became an isolation hospital for typhus casualties, and in the second half of the nineteenth century, a military prison. Today the island is the home of the Armdale Yacht Club. Anyone who died on Melville Island was buried on nearby Deadmans Island. For many years the cemetery was neglected. In 1907, businessman Charles Longley bought the island and set up an amusement park, which closed in 1927. Three years later, A. J. Davis purchased the island and opened a pleasure park. Deadmans Island changed hands again in the later 1930s. Subsequent owners found skeletons, resulting more recently in the restoration of the island as a burial ground.

In 1908, Scottish-born Sir Sandford Fleming, a prominent engineer and inventor, donated to the public ninety-five acres (thirty-eight hectares) of his large estate near the head of the Northwest Arm. Sir Sandford Fleming Park, commonly known as the Dingle, immediately attracted Haligonians. Fleming also had a tower erected there to commemorate 150 years of representative government in the province. It opened in 1912, offering a further attraction.

On the eastern side of the Arm, Point Pleasant Park was for many years part of the Halifax defence system. The entrance to the channel was guarded by gun batteries and, in times of war, by a chain boom across the water that was anchored to a ring in a rock on the park's shore. Far out on the western side, York Redoubt defended the approaches to Halifax Harbour.

Also on the eastern side, several large estates were established in the 1800s by wealthy residents, including businessmen, politicians, and judges. Between these properties and Point Pleasant Park stood the Northwest Arm Penitentiary, since demolished. In the twentieth century, several private recreational clubs opened on the shores of the former estates, and their grounds have mostly given way to residential streets.

With all this activity, it became desirable to have some form of communication between Halifax peninsula and the far side of the Northwest Arm. Over the years, ferries have carried passengers from at least seven locations—today known as Point Pleasant Park, Oaklands Estate, Oakland Road, South Street, Coburg Road, Jubilee Road, and Quinpool Road—across the narrow inlet. The boat launch site at Jubilee Road is all that remains of an early ferry across the Arm. An 1817 sketch by J. E. Woolford shows the ferry ready to leave for Melville Island. An attempt was made to revive this ferry in 2019, when professional mariner David Backman offered a rush-hour service from Fleming Park to commuters wishing to avoid the heavy traffic into Halifax. A new dock was to be built at the Jubilee Road side. The ferry operated for a short time, but the following year the COVID-19 pandemic put an end to work in downtown Halifax. The ferry ceased to operate.

Another ferry ran for some years across the Arm between the village of Jollimore and a landing at William Cunard's Oaklands Estate. But when Halifax businessman Roderick MacDonald bought the estate in 1904, he did not allow the ferry to continue. In compensation, residents requested an extension of what would become Oakland Road as far as the Arm. A solution was reached when MacDonald provided an access point farther north, although in 1913 MacDonald closed the Oaklands access point altogether. A further petition requesting an Oakland Road extension was successful, and a new ferry dock was built.

The Jollimore ferry began service between the foot of Oakland Road and the new Fleming Park soon after the park's establishment in 1912. In that era, few people had independent means of transportation. The ferry carried Haligonians wanting to escape the city on a hot summer's day to the Dingle beach and its woodland trails. A ferry also carried passengers to the Dingle from the foot of Quinpool Road in the 1930s and 1940s.

In 1913, Josiah Boutilier took over from Sam Jollimore a ferry to Fleming Park, which departed at the foot of South Street. Boutilier then applied to operate a ferry from a new dock at the foot of Oakland Road. He ran this ferry to a landing dock near the Memorial Tower at the Dingle until he retired in 1948. His sons Fred and Foster took over the operation until the early 1960s, and the ferry ceased operations in 1965. In the 1970s, the Oakland Road dock was closed to the public and became dilapidated. In the 1980s, adjacent resident and former Halifax mayor Leonard Kitz campaigned to have the City of Halifax rebuild the dock for public use; this was eventually successful. A second round of improvements to the dock and landing—new steps and lighting—was completed in early 2013. Then MLA for Halifax Atlantic Michèle Raymond attempted to re-establish the Oakland Road ferry, having it operate on a trial basis for two weeks in 2001 and again in 2002; however, the service proved commercially unviable. The dock is maintained today as a public access point to the Northwest Arm.

Much earlier, Charles Longley operated a private ferry to service his amusement park on Deadmans Island. That ferry ride included the price of park admission. The Saraguay Club, which for some time was accessible only by water, offered another private service for the convenience of its members. It ran from the Pine Hill property (now the Atlantic School of Theology). Those wishing to cross would blow a horn to summon the ferry operator, who would then row across to pick them up. When a good road was built along the Arm, the ferry became redundant.

Improved roads around the Arm and the increasing use of cars in the twentieth century heralded the demise of these old ferries. The last one to survive into the twentieth century was operated by the Purcell family from 1853 until 1971. It ran between Purcells Cove and Point Pleasant Park, where today Purcell's Landing marks its eastern terminus.

PUBNICO HARBOUR

Pubnico is one of Nova Scotia's oldest communities. It was founded by Philippe Mius d'Entremont in 1654, when Governor Charles de Saint-Étienne de La Tour gave him a large grant of land extending from Cape Negro to Cape Forchu, along with the title of baron. D'Entremont made his home on the east side of what is now Pubnico Harbour, where he built a manor house. There with his wife, Madeleine, they raised their family. With the help of his employees, he cleared and cultivated the land around his house. When he was appointed king's attorney, he moved to Port-Royal, and his oldest son, Jacques, managed his property and inherited the title of baron.

Jacques, his brother Abraham, and their families remained in Pubnico until the Expulsion that began in 1755. When Acadians were allowed to return to Nova Scotia in the 1760s, they came back to find that their land on the east side of the harbour was now in the hands of the English. They re-established the Acadian population on the west side of the harbour, and the community of West Pubnico is now the centre of Acadian culture in the region.

Today, there are settlements on both sides of the harbour, designated in true Nova Scotian fashion East and West Pubnico, with all the variations of Pubnico: Middle West, Middle East, Lower Middle West, Lower East Pubnico, and so on. A few of these communities today are largely anglophone, but the majority of residents around the harbour in East and West Pubnico remain proudly Acadian. Of course, now there are good roads around the harbour, but in 1914 the inhabitants felt the need for better communication between

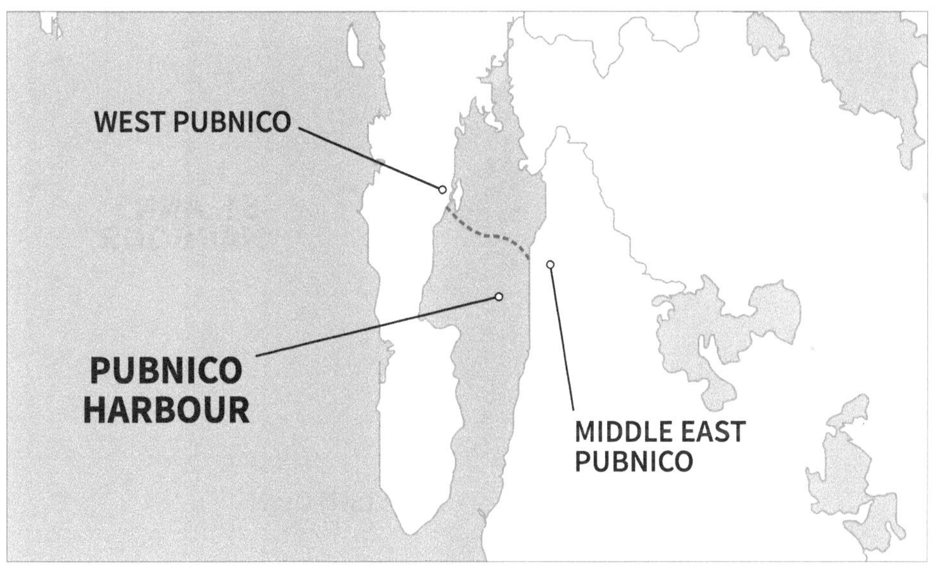

Middle West and Middle East Pubnico. They sent a petition to the Argyle Township County Court with many signatories, requesting a ferry service across the harbour and recommending Arthur d'Entremont as the operator. The request was granted, and Arthur was duly appointed ferry operator by the warden, Arthur Sim, on May 5, 1914. The fee for crossing and returning was set at the standard twenty cents. Today motorized traffic round the head of the harbour has rendered the service redundant.

ST. ANNS HARBOUR

There is a long history of European presence at St. Anns Harbour. In 1629, a French sea captain, Charles Daniel, came to the harbour with a group of Scottish prisoners who were tasked with building a fort before they were transported to England. Daniel left his men to garrison the fort. He returned with more settlers to establish the settlement of what was initially called Havre Sainte Anne. After the garrison was transferred to Newfoundland, a handful

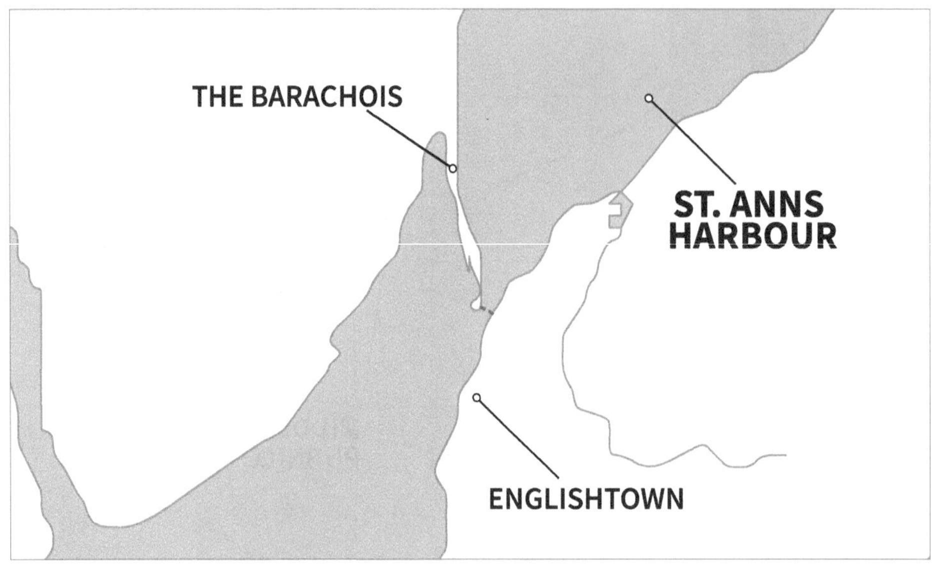

of civilians remained in the French settlement, making their living by fishing and trading with the Mi'kmaq.

In the early 1650s, the harbour was home to a fishing station operated by Simon Denys, whose brother Nicolas ran the fishery at St. Peters, also in Île-Royale, as Cape Breton was known then by French colonists. The Denys brothers were captured by agents of their bitter enemy, Charles de Menou d'Aulnay, who took them as prisoners to Quebec, where Simon remained. The early fishery at Sainte Anne was abandoned.

The next wave of settlers did not arrive until 1713, when control of mainland Nova Scotia was ceded to the British, leaving the French with Île-Royale. Ste Anne was one of the harbours to be fortified, and its Fort Dauphin was considered for the site of the main fortress that would eventually be constructed at Louisbourg. Fort Dauphin was manned by soldiers from Newfoundland, and a barracks, forge, and lime kiln were set up. Gypsum was mined at the head of the harbour, and fishing continued as a main occupation. After the final capture of Louisbourg in 1758 by British forces, the community of Sainte Anne was destroyed.

Meanwhile, in the late 1700s, a wave of Scottish immigrants arrived in the harbour and settled near the site of the former French fort, across the narrow channel from the sandbar that protects the harbour. These arrivals spoke English, and their settlement became known as Englishtown. They farmed and fished like their neighbours, and enough of them owned boats that they could easily cross the channel to the sandbar, named officially St. Anns Beach, but locally known today as the barachois.

The best-known resident of Englishtown was Angus MacAskill, the son of a farming family that came to Cape Breton in 1831 when he was a young boy. As a teenager he grew increasingly taller and stronger, until in his twenties at the height of seven feet nine inches he was considered a giant. He went on tour in the 1840s and returned with enough money saved to buy a farm and a gristmill. He also ran a store. MacAskill died in 1863.

It was not until 1819 that some Gaelic-speaking Scottish Presbyterian settlers arrived in the harbour—now anglicized to St. Anns—led by Norman McLeod, their minister. McLeod, known to be rigid and intolerant, ruled the community with an iron fist, until the failure of the potato crop and the lax ways of residents caused him to leave with some followers for New Zealand.

In the mid-nineteenth century, a ferry across the narrow channel from Englishtown to the barachois was operated by members of the MacLean family, whose descendants continued to run the service for over 150 years. Today, a provincial cable ferry, the *Torquil MacLean*, commemorates the most recent family member. It replaced the previous ferry, the *Angus MacAskill*, in 2010. Up to fifteen cars can drive from the ramp straight onto the ferry's deck, and up to ninety-five passengers along with the two crew can cross the channel in just a few minutes. The ferry runs year-round, around the clock, except when ice floes interrupt service. In an unfortunate incident in 2013, a man drowned when he drove his car off the end of the ferry.

An earlier iteration of the Englishtown ferry. [NS ARCHIVES, CLARA DENNIS 1981-541 NUMBER 415CB]

Today's Englishtown ferry. [TONY WEBSTER VIA WIKIMEDIA COMMONS]

SYDNEY HARBOUR

Sydney Harbour, already familiar to the Mi'kmaq, was known to early European fishers as Baie des Espagnols, or Spanish Bay. It was so named because Spanish vessels visited the harbour every summer in the late sixteenth

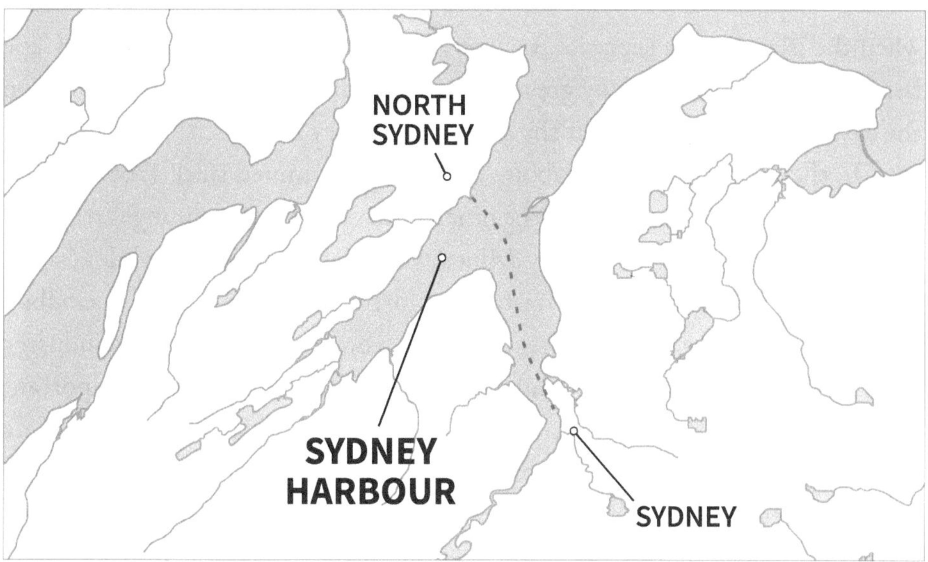

and early seventeenth centuries to fish and trade with the Indigenous inhabitants. In 1713 by the Treaty of Utrecht, after years of disputes over territory in North America, France ceded mainland Nova Scotia to Britain, retaining Île-Royale (Cape Breton Island). The harbour gained importance to colonists in the eighteenth century with the development of the Fortress of Louisbourg. At this time, a small garrison of French soldiers guarded the port, which was frequented by vessels from France and the port of Quebec as well as by shipping from the Atlantic coast.

In the 1740s, a group of Acadians came to Spanish Bay from the mainland to avoid deportation. Most of them left soon afterward because of the area's poor farming conditions. With the fall of Quebec in 1760 and the loss of French territory, including Île-Royale, the area came under British control, although it was not initially resettled.

It was not until the mid-1780s that Cape Breton's newly appointed governor, Joseph Frederick Wallet DesBarres, brought a shipload of destitute British settlers into Sydney Harbour. DesBarres left after a short time. These settlers were followed by a contingent of Loyalists, who formed the nucleus of the population of the town of Sydney, which served as its capital. (During the period when the island was a separate province, Sydney served as the capital of Cape Breton.) The town of Sydney grew up on the South Arm, which is situated on the east side of Spanish Bay at the mouth of Sydney River.

On the west side of the harbour, coal had been mined since 1766 and was shipped from a nearby wharf. In the nineteenth century, the mining settlement that became the town of Sydney Mines was established. Meanwhile, North Sydney was developing on the harbour's North West Arm, where a sandbar, known as the North Bar, protected the harbour. A shipbuilding industry grew up on Sydney Harbour, and North Sydney soon became an important commercial port. Settlers from Scotland came to work in the region where employment opportunities were plentiful. Coal from the area's mines and iron ore from Newfoundland's Bell Island became the basis for the industry that started in Sydney in 1901 with the opening of the Dominion Iron and Steel Company steel plant.

With the burgeoning population, travel between the communities around the harbour became essential. In 1844, the legislative assembly received a request of support for a steam ferry from Sydney to Sydney River to meet the steam packet that was planned to run from Halifax to Newfoundland, calling at North Sydney. The original vessel, the steamer *North America*, was replaced just two years later by the more expensive *Unicorn*, and the operators were, unsurprisingly, seeking an increased provincial subsidy.

By the late 1850s, a regular ferry service ran between North Sydney and Sydney. Originally managed by private boat owners, the service was taken over by the newly named Cape Breton Electrical Company, which had been incorporated in 1900 and operated the ferry from its wharf in North Sydney. Travellers who arrived in Cape Breton on the interprovincial ferry from Port aux Basques, NL, could then cross to Sydney.

The eventual construction of bridges at the head of the North West and South Arms, significant improvement in roads, and the increased use of motorized vehicles made travel around Sydney Harbour by car much faster and easier than waiting for a ferry. The service was discontinued. A bus service now links Sydney, North Sydney, and Sydney Mines.

The North Sydney Cape Breton Electric Company ferry terminal, North Sydney, NS. [NS ARCHIVES]

COUNTRY HARBOUR

Originally known by its Mi'kmaw name of Moukodome, or port of Mocodome, Country Harbour on the province's Eastern Shore is the long estuary of the Country Harbour River. Together with neighbouring Isaacs Harbour, they form one of the province's widest estuaries. The settlement of Country Harbour was granted to disbanded soldiers after the American Revolution, but the settlers had an inauspicious start. They arrived in the winter of 1783/84 in two ships that carried supplies. The first arrived safely, but the second ship was delayed by storms and lost a deck-load of lumber on its journey. The new arrivals hastily built log cabins that proved inadequate to withstand the cold weather. Many men died; the survivors were helped by Mi'kmaw inhabitants. The settlement on the northeast side of the harbour became known as Mount Misery.

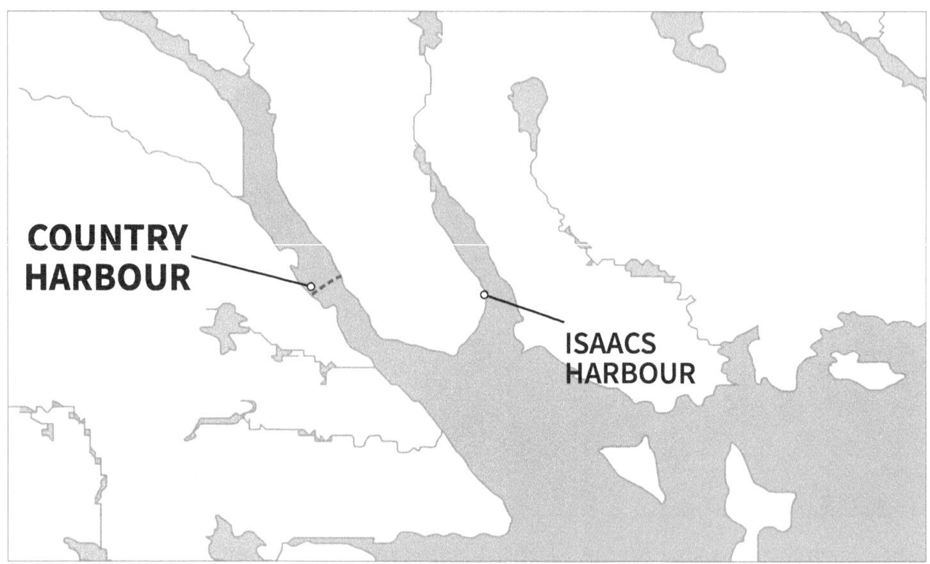

Some of the survivors left as soon as they were able, while those who remained became farmers, lumber workers, or fishers. They lived in scattered properties on the river until Captain John Leggett established a settlement behind Mount Misery, where he operated a store. He was joined by other settlers who ran various businesses—stores, a tannery, a carding mill, and a sawmill that exported lumber. The village took the name of Stormont.

The area settlers experienced more adversity when a hurricane destroyed homes and ships. Consequently, most people gave up and moved away. One family left behind an employee, Isaac Webb, who moved with his family to what became known as Isaacs Harbour. In the 1830s, they were joined by other families, and a successful shipbuilding industry developed there and in Country Harbour.

The 1860s saw a short-lived gold rush, which fuelled the economy of Isaacs Harbour and left behind abandoned mines. There were also mines on Country Harbour. Sporadic attempts to revive the industry have failed. Since the 1860s the population has dwindled. Some residents still make their living from fishing; deep-sea fishing vessels come to the head of Country Harbour to transfer their catch to trucks. Even today, Country Harbour is sparsely populated, mostly by retired people. A few residents commute to work in larger communities.

Although one might expect there to have been ferry services in the nineteenth century, the fluctuating population seems never to have stabilized sufficiently to warrant one. Today, a provincially run ferry across the mouth of Country Harbour serves travellers along the Eastern Shore coastal road that passes through Port Bickerton. It is named *Theodore O'Hara,* after Port Bickerton's first lighthouse keeper. The cable ferry carries fifteen vehicles and runs every fifteen minutes in summer, every half hour for the rest of the year when conditions permit. There are no communities at either terminus.

3
Island Ferries

The many islands off Nova Scotia's lengthy coast were well-known to the Mi'kmaq, for whom canoes were the regular mode of travel as they moved from the forest to the coast each summer, and perhaps pitched their wigwams on the islands. As early as the sixteenth century, some European fishing crews used island beaches to dry their catch. The fishers from different countries traditionally came to the same area each summer, but it would be some time before offshore islands became permanent fishing bases, and even later that mixed economies developed there.

The large island of Cape Breton, known to the Mi'kmaq as Unama'ki (land of fog), and for many years governed by France and known as Île-Royale, became part of Nova Scotia after the Treaty of Paris was signed in 1763, and the territory was officially ceded to Britain. Until the opening of the Canso Causeway in 1955, many ferries have connected it with the mainland across the Strait of Canso. Several smaller islands off Nova Scotia's coast are also served by ferries. When settlers in search of land discovered the economic potential of the province's islands, they requested grants. Subsequently, fishing villages and small offshore farming settlements grew up. As the populations of the island communities increased, so too did residents feel an increased need for regular communication with the mainland. Enterprising boat owners offered ferry services, seeking licences from the counties in which the islands lay. Subsidies for operation from the legislative assembly became established.

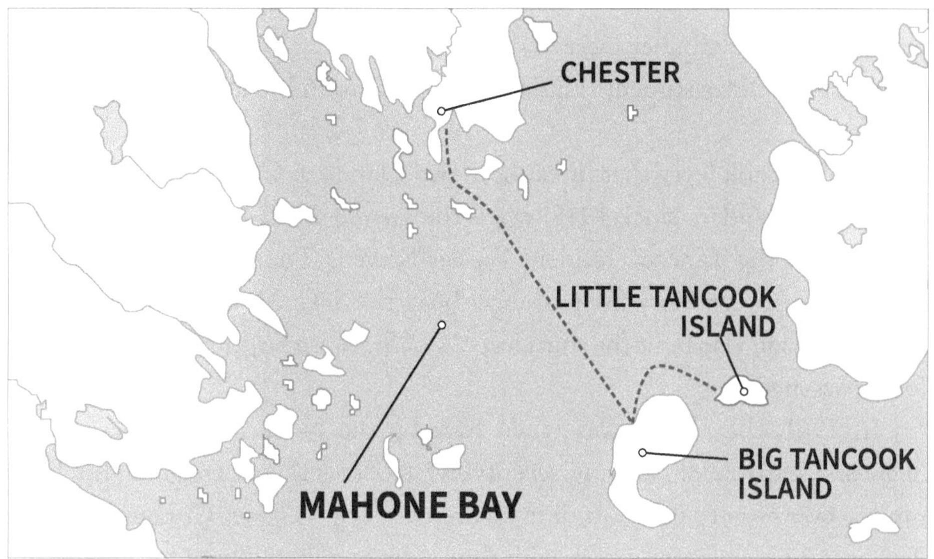

THE TANCOOK ISLANDS

Big and Little Tancook are among the many islands that populate Mahone Bay in Nova Scotia's South Shore region. Families from Lunenburg settled on these islands in the 1790s and early 1800s. Most settled on Big Tancook, while the smaller island became home to the Levy family. By the end of the century, the farming settlers of Big Tancook had acquired a reputation for growing cabbages that they preserved as sauerkraut, some for their own use and some for market on the mainland. Many island residents also made a living by fishing and boatbuilding. Amos Stevens's Tancook whalers found a ready market. By the late nineteenth century, Big Tancook was densely populated, with a Baptist church and a school to serve its more than five hundred residents.

The once-flourishing sauerkraut industry suffered a setback in the twentieth century when an invasion of white-tailed deer began to graze on the cabbage fields. Commercial sauerkraut manufacture moved to the mainland, followed by the boatbuilding industry. Residents also moved to the mainland, and now the population has dwindled to a little over one hundred. The island's elementary school risked closure when its student numbers dropped to two or three, but the number increased to eight in the 2023–24 year, keeping the school open. Older students take the ferry year-round to attend school on the mainland.

The Tancook ferry that links these two islands to Chester has been a lifeline to the islanders since 1935, when the *Gerald L. C.* came into service. It was built by Big Tancook resident Wesley Stevens. Four years later, the ferry was replaced by a twenty-five passenger boat, the *S. G. Mason,* built by Stanley Mason. Mason also built the third ferry, *T. J. Service,* a larger vessel that carried forty passengers.

In 1961, the service was taken over by the Nova Scotia government's *Shoreham,* capable of carrying seventy-five passengers and freight. This ferry ran for over twenty years, until it was replaced by *William G. Ernst* in 1982. This was a much larger vessel, with four crew members, space for ninety-two passengers, and a crane to load freight. It has since been refitted with a hydraulic crane. In summer, the ferry brings tourists to the islands, but the aging vessel has had its passenger capacity reduced to forty-five.

The *William G. Ernst* was due to be retired in the mid-2020s and replaced by a new ferry from Blandford. Delays have made the date that the new ferry will come into service uncertain. For now, the *William G. Ernst* is still the only link between the Tancooks and the mainland. It is slated to carry eighteen cars as well as passengers and freight.

CAPE SABLE ISLAND

At the southernmost tip of Nova Scotia, Cape Sable Island was once part of the extensive area known simply as Cape Sable, which from the 1620s was the domain of Charles de Saint-Étienne de La Tour. La Tour and a few companions had remained at Port-Royal when most of the settlers returned to France in 1607. He later spent some years roaming the forests of Acadie until he turned his attention to the Cape Sable area. He built Fort St. Louis at what is now

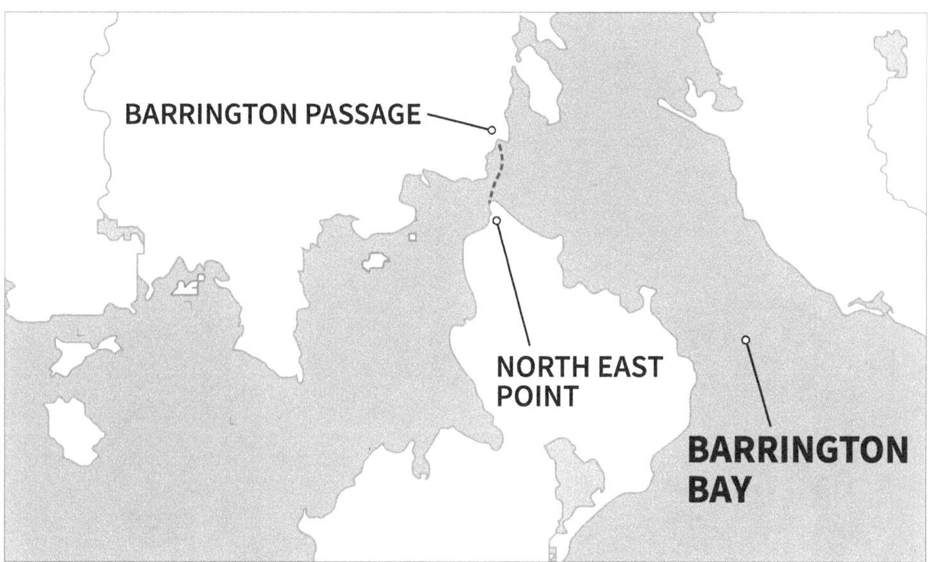

Port La Tour. This became the base for his fishing and fur-trading activities, which extended over much of southwestern Nova Scotia until 1641, when the area was seized by Charles de Menou d'Aulnay.

In 1710, Port-Royal, then the capital of Acadie, was ceded to the British, and the Treaty of Utrecht in 1713 documented the British conquest of the rest of what would become mainland Nova Scotia. With the Expulsion of the Acadians from Cape Sable Island in 1759, the island became a destination for British settlers from the New England colonies. Fishers from Cape Cod were familiar with the waters in the nearby Gulf of Maine, so from 1760 many of them took up Governor Charles Lawrence's offer of free land on the island.

Among the early English settlers was Archelaus Smith, a tanner, fisher, and surveyor, who came first to Barrington in 1760. He and his family then moved to Cape Sable Island in 1773. They acquired extensive land in the north of the island and established their home on a cove (now McGrays Cove), near today's Centreville. Cape Sable Island's local history museum is named after Smith.

Fishing remained the chief occupation of settlers, some of whom also became boatbuilders. In about 1905, they created the fishing boats called Cape

A car aboard the ferry to Cape Sable Island, NS. [NS ARCHIVES, CLARA DENNIS 1981-541 NUMBER 2]

Islanders, now used by fishers across the province. These boats are known for their flat, keeled bottom at the stern and rounded bow, and are particularly popular with lobster fishers. Boatbuilding is still carried on from Cape Sable Island today. The lobster fishery is also a major sector of the economy, along with seafood processing and marketing.

In the early twentieth century, not all the residents had access to a boat, and from the 1920s a ferry was operated by the Barrington and Cape Island Steam Ferry Company between the island and the mainland. It was replaced in 1949 by a causeway between Barrington Passage on the mainland and Cape Sable Island's community of North East Point.

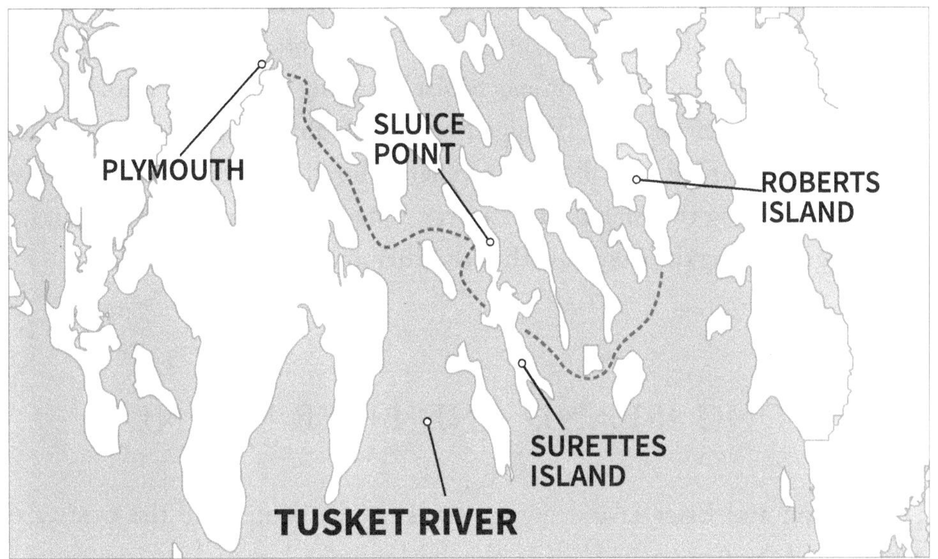

TUSKET RIVER ISLANDS

The Tusket River is a major waterway with multiple branches coursing through southwest Nova Scotia in what is today Yarmouth County. The Mi'kmaq were well acquainted with the islands at the mouth of the Tusket River, which offered ample fishing. In the seventeenth century, the same islands became well-known to French fishers and fur traders. The islands were claimed as part of Charles de Saint-Étienne de La Tour's Cape Sable domain, and he established a trading post on Roberts Island early in the century. (The island was still known to Acadians into the twentieth century as Île de La Tour.) In the 1760s, settlers from New England were granted land on the islands to which they gave their names. Some Acadians who had returned from exile and found their former farmland around the Minas Basin occupied by New Englanders also settled on the Tusket Islands. All the colonists of the islands depended mainly on fishing for their livelihood.

Those residents of the islands around the Tusket River estuary were isolated from communities that were only short distances across the water. They sent petitions to the warden and councillors of the municipality of Argyle, dating from the middle of the nineteenth century. In 1868, they requested that ferry services should be established between Roberts Island and Morris (Surettes) Island, and from Thomas Muise's landing on Morris Island to the mainland on the south side. The signatories were almost all Acadians. These requests were granted and allowed travellers who did not own boats to move more freely among the islands. Today, ferries have been replaced by highways and bridges linking the islands with each other and the town of Tusket.

LONG ISLAND AND BRIER ISLAND

Long Island and Brier Island, in southwest Nova Scotia, are the westward extension of the Annapolis Valley's North Mountain. Long Island is separated from Digby Neck by Petit Passage, and from Brier Island by Grand Passage. Originally, the Mi'kmaq came to these islands in summer to gather shellfish. Subsequently, Samuel de Champlain noted the islands and the passages between them when he accompanied Pierre Dugua de Monts on his exploratory expedition to what would become Acadie in 1604.

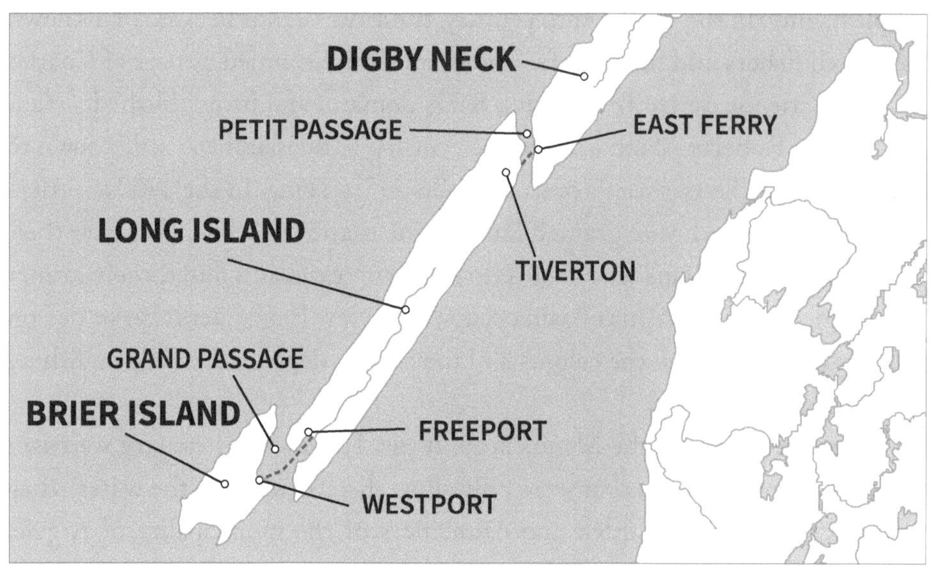

The first European settlers on the islands were a group of New England fishers and their families, who arrived in the 1760s at the invitation of Governor Charles Lawrence. They were joined in 1783 by Loyalist families, including the Blackfords, who were among the early settlers on Digby Neck. Initially, the residents used their own boats to travel between the islands, but in the nineteenth century, as fewer residents owned boats and travel became more frequent, ferries were established.

PETIT PASSAGE

The waters of Petit Passage are particularly turbulent because they are influenced by the Bay of Fundy's tides, ranked the world's largest. Early ferry operators could safely row their wooden boats between East Ferry and Tiverton only during periods of slack water at high and low tide.

The first ferry across Petit Passage was run from the eastern side by Martin Blackford, who received his licence in 1804. The ferry was no longer operating in 1847, but it was revived by 1851, when two unnamed ferry operators, one on each side, received grants of two pounds ten shillings each. One of them may have been a member of the Blackford family, as a year later Martin Blackford's sons Anthony, Joseph, and Israel were operating the ferry. The service would remain mostly in the Blackford family for many years. In 1857, Anthony Blackford and Samuel Outhouse were ferry operators.

Anthony Blackford's son Israel ran the ferry for some time. He was replaced by David Scott in 1873. The residents of East Ferry petitioned the Court of General Sessions for the reinstatement of Israel, who, they wrote, "performed his duties for a number of years when the travel was so small that it paid almost nothing and as soon as the Ferry paid anything Mr. Blackford was deprived of it, and as he has had a long experience and is well fitted for the duties of Ferryman, we humbly pray your Honorable Court to give our Petition a favourable consideration..." Their request was granted; Israel resumed his duties.

In 1880, Scott was again appointed to run ferries from both sides. He was replaced in 1886 by Henry Alline Blackford, followed by his son, Byron

The car ferry to Tiverton, NS, carrying passengers across the Petit Passage, August 1950. [NS ARCHIVES, ALEXANDER H. LEIGHTON 1988-413 NEGATIVE NUMBER 9-D]

Blackford two years later. At that time, the fare was set at twenty-five cents per passenger, forty-five cents for a horse, seventy-five cents for a horse and carriage, with varying prices for different kinds of livestock. Rates were also set for goods.

Byron Blackford oversaw the modernization of the Petit Passage ferry. In 1888, local residents petitioned the government for a steam ferry. Their request was received favourably, and the following year Blackford was operating a steamer across Petit Passage. As well as passengers, the vessel carried horses and cattle. Blackford continued as ferry operator and was supported by government grants. A second steam ferry took over the service in 1899.

For some reason, in the early twentieth century, government regulations required that the mail be carried by oars and sail. This impractical rule was usually disregarded, but when an official inspector arrived, Blackford brought his sailboat to East Ferry and loaded the mail and the inspector on board. When the current threatened to sweep the boat away, Blackford hailed a nearby gasoline-powered boat—contrary to regulations—and they were towed to safety. After this near disaster, the regulations were changed so that gasoline-powered boats were permitted to transport the mail. Byron Blackford continued to operate the ferry for many years, using a series of boats. The provincial government took over the service in 1946. Blackford died shortly after, in 1950.

The current ferry across the five-minute Petit Passage route between East Ferry and Long Island's Tiverton is called *Petit Princess*. It carries twenty-four cars and ninety-five passengers plus four crew, runs hourly, and costs seven dollars for a return trip.

GRAND PASSAGE

The wider channel between Long Island and Brier Island is known as Grand Passage. George Morrell of Westport, son of one of the early settlers on Brier Island, is said to have initiated the first ferry at Grand Passage in 1817, although the first official record shows James Peters receiving a licence as a ferry operator in 1822. He was succeeded three years later by James Titus. In 1826, Morrell moved across Grand Passage to Freeport on Long Island and began to operate a ferry from that side. From 1857, with a few exceptions, the ferry licence remained in the Morrell family for many years. For a time, a second ferry was run by the Peters family from Brier Island. These early ferries were propelled by oar or sail until 1896, when a steam ferry was introduced. Ralph Morrell, who operated the ferry from Freeport in the early twentieth century, replaced the steam ferry with a gasoline-operated vessel in 1905. It ran until 1919, when

Grand Passage ferry arriving at Freeport, NS, November 1950. [NS ARCHIVES, ALEXANDER H. LEIGHTON 1988-413 NEGATIVE NUMBER 2688-D]

it was crushed in a collision with a steamer. The engine was salvaged and used in a replacement ferry.

Ralph Morrell died in 1933, and the licence was taken over by his widow, who employed Arthur Sullivan to operate the ferry. By 1936, residents were asking for improvements to keep up with the growing demand for transport of cars and trucks. In response, ferry slips were improved to allow vehicles to be loaded onto scows, which were towed across the water by a small boat with a single-cylinder, gasoline-powered engine.

With an increasing number of cars on the roads, the Digby municipal council requested that the provincial government take over operation of the ferries at both Grand and Petit Passages. Action was delayed, likely because of wartime priorities, until 1946, when ferries owned and operated by the Department of Highways became part of the highway system.

The name of the Grand Passage boat that came into service for the eight-minute route between Freeport on Long Island and Westport on Brier Island in 2016 is *Margaret's Justice*. The name commemorates a widow, Margaret Hubbard, who walked from Brier Island to Halifax to successfully establish her claim to land on Brier and Long Islands. This ferry has a capacity of eighteen vehicles and ninety-five passengers. Today, the ferries between Digby Neck and Brier Island depart at regularly scheduled hours.

PICTOU ISLAND

Pictou Island lies in the Northumberland Strait, 5 miles (7.5 kilometres) from Caribou Ferry on the mainland, north of Pictou town. The island was once a traditional summer meeting place among the Mi'kmaq. Scottish settlers came to the island in the late eighteenth century. They cleared land for small farms and fished in the strait.

In 1809, Pictou Island was granted to the Royal Navy's Admiral Sir Alexander Inglis Cochrane, who was visiting the town of Pictou. Cochrane, who remained an active and prominent naval officer, may never have lived on his island property. He retained an interest in it, but it was left to the Scottish settlers to develop its resources. The first group of settlers were Roman Catholics who had come from the island of Barra, in the Outer Hebrides. They formed what was known as the Barra Settlement in 1802. These people, who were mostly fishers, were joined in 1817 by Irish families sent by the admiral

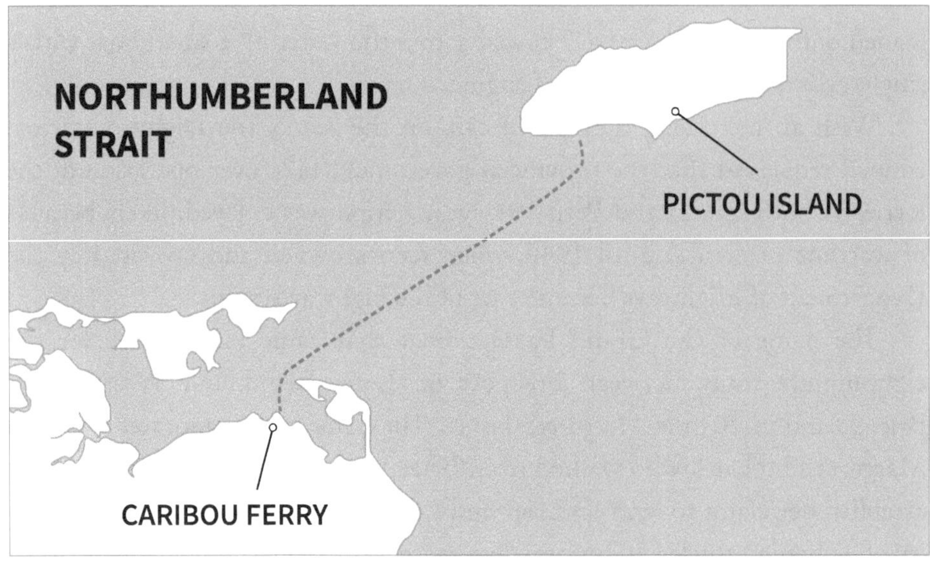

to establish farms on the island. The fishery, however, remained the island's economic base into the twentieth century, and canneries were established to process the catch.

In the mid-twentieth century, the island was well populated. Farming and fishing remained the chief occupations. Many year-round residents have since moved to the mainland. Summer residents augment the population for a few months every year, when the weather is perhaps at its best.

Although boat owners made the crossing to the mainland from Pictou Island at their convenience when they, or their neighbours, needed to travel, fishers had other priorities. The residents needed a formal ferry service. One was finally established in the early twentieth century and has been running for more than one hundred years. The service has always been a seasonal operation, as winter conditions with ice in the Northumberland Strait make the crossing by boat impossible.

Today, Pictou Island Charters runs a motor vessel, *Cetacean Search*, from May until November. The ferry carries passengers, baggage, and freight, including bicycles, but no cars. The crossing runs from the dock at Caribou Ferry and takes about forty-five minutes to reach the island. This is Nova Scotia's only remaining privately owned ferry.

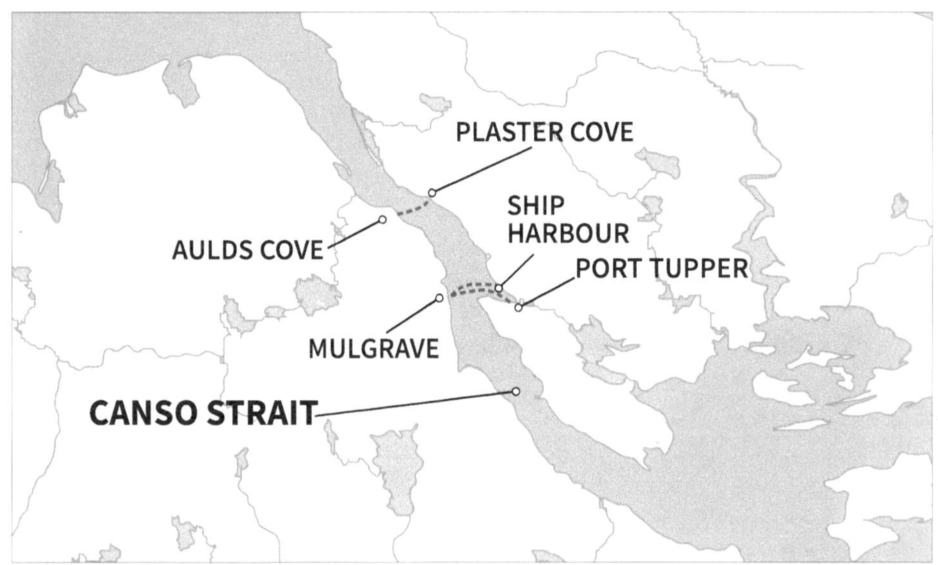

CAPE BRETON ISLAND

Cape Breton Island has not always been part of Nova Scotia. Formerly known as Île-Royale, it was part of French colonial territory in North America until the end of the Seven Years War in 1763, when the French surrendered their claims to land in Canada. Although it is now linked to the mainland by the Canso Causeway, Cape Breton was once served by a series of ferries across the Strait of Canso.

Early communities on both sides of the strait made their living from lumbering, fishing, and shipbuilding. McNairs Cove (known as Mulgrave from 1859), on the western mainland shore, was settled in 1800 by Loyalists, who initially relied on lumbering before turning to fishing. Ship Harbour on the island side of the strait developed as a fishing and shipbuilding community. As early as 1819, ferries were crossing the strait. In 1833, a passenger ferry ran from Mulgrave to Ship Harbour (now Port Hawkesbury) on the strait's eastern shore.

A postcard showing the Mulgrave, NS, ferry wharves, ca. 1909, published by Canadian Souvenir Post Card, Warwick Bros. & Rutter Limited Publishers, Toronto. [NS ARCHIVES]

By the mid-nineteenth century, several ferries were operating across the Strait of Canso. On the island side, Ship Harbour was the base for a ferry that Hugh McMillan was operating between Aulds Cove and Plaster Cover (Port Hastings) from 1819. He was still in business ten years later, when he asked for an increased subsidy from the legislative assembly. In 1844, he received a grant of twenty pounds.

In 1847, there were two ferries in operation. McMillan's ran to McNairs Cove from Ship Harbour, while McPherson's crossed from Steep Creek, closer to Canso, to the island shore. McMillan, the Ship Harbour ferry operator, was unhappy because he had to split the grant with a ferry operator on the mainland. A further cause for complaint was the increased frequency of the mail service: the postman now had to be ferried across twice a week, creating extra work for McMillan.

The ferry steamer John Cabot *entering the Port Hawkesbury, NS, dock.*
[NS ARCHIVES]

Ferry operators continued to petition the assembly for assistance throughout the 1850s. Some ferries ran between Ship Harbour and Aulds Cove, others from McNairs Cove. Ferry traffic increased as more people travelled for business or pleasure, and steam-powered ferry boats came into use in the 1860s. With the development of railways on the mainland and Cape Breton Island, a train ferry was established across the strait from Mulgrave to a railway dock at Port Tupper. Initially, in 1894, passengers were carried on the SS *Mulgrave,* while rail cars were towed on a wooden barge. In 1901, passenger and freight cars crossed the strait on SS *Scotia I,* which was replaced in its turn by the larger SS *Scotia II* in 1915.

In 1902, Isaac Embree of Port Hawkesbury was operating a ferry across the strait. His son, Captain James Embree, initiated the first car-carrying ferry in 1913. In 1922, the *Edith C. Walker*, thought to be the strait's first steam-powered car ferry, was operated by Captain P. J. Walker. Four years later, the Nova Scotia government's Department of Highways took over the service across the Canso Strait with its ferry boat *Pont de Canseau*, which was succeeded in 1927 by the *Breton*. The following year, the *Sir Charles Tupper* came into service, carrying up to eighteen cars. During the day, the fares were $1.25 for a car, and $0.20 for a passenger, but from midnight until 7:00 a.m. fares doubled. In winter, when ice blocked the dock at Port Hawkesbury, ferries were rerouted to Point Tupper.

Increasing commercial and tourist traffic in the twentieth century resulted in long lineups for the ferry service between the island and the mainland. In 1952, a contract was awarded for the construction of a causeway to replace it. The Canso Causeway opened in 1955, and ferry service across the strait ended.

ISLE MADAME

Isle Madame and its surrounding islands, off Cape Breton's southeastern coast, had been known to European fishers for many years before settlements were established. The main island was used as a base by Basque fishing vessels, possibly as early as the sixteenth century. Permanent fishing villages grew up in the early eighteenth century, when France lost Acadie to Britain and set about developing its remaining territory of Île-Royale. The island is thought to be named for Madame de Maintenon, the second wife of Louis XIV.

The French inhabitants of Isle Madame were eventually deported, along with Acadians, after the fall of Louisbourg in 1745. A few families who had escaped from Port Toulouse (St. Peters) on Cape Breton later made their way back to the island. They were joined in 1766 by Acadians who had returned from exile in New England.

Also in the 1760s, two men from Jersey in the British Channel Islands, Charles and John Robin, came to Isle Madame and started a fishery on what became known as Jerseyman Island. They suffered a setback during the American Revolution, when their wharves and warehouses were raided and sacked by the notorious naval officer John Paul Jones, but they recovered and

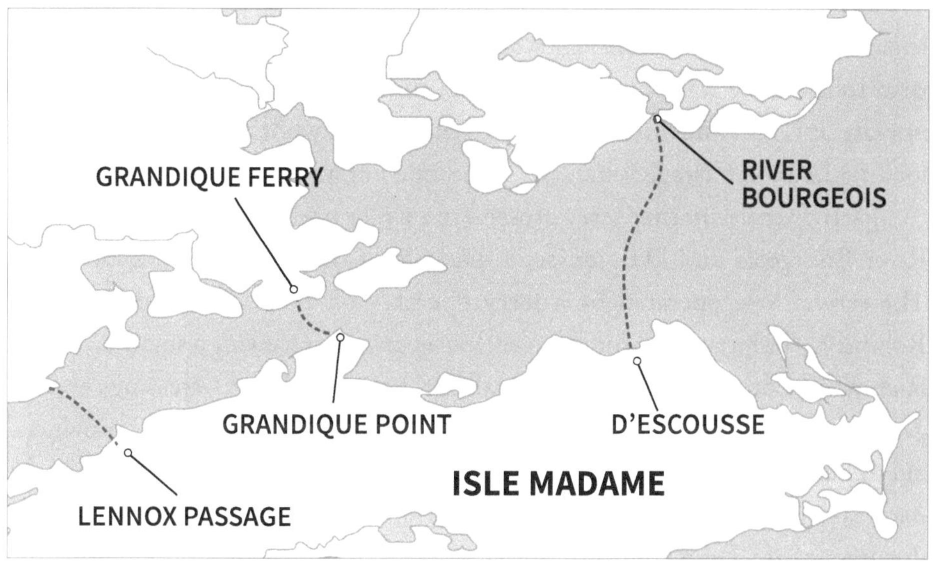

established a successful operation based on the harbour at Arichat, on Isle Madame. It would grow into an extensive business, employing hundreds of fishers and workers in processing plants on Cape Breton and the Gaspé Peninsula.

Fisheries were established on other islands as well. French merchants and fishers came to Petit-de-Grat from Canso in 1718; however, they were forced out, and the settlement was destroyed after the fall of Louisbourg. Settlement resumed in the 1760s. John Janvrin, also a Jersey merchant, initially established a fishery at Arichat in partnership with his two brothers. He later received a grant of the island that bears his name, where he set up a successful fishing station.

Fishing continued to be the mainstay of Isle Madame's economy for many years. The island's economy suffered like that of other places when the cod fishery collapsed at the end of the twentieth century. Since then, the fishery has diversified and is still an important industry there.

For many years, travel among the islands was necessarily by boat. In the early nineteenth century, ferries across Lennox Passage linked Isle Madame to the mainland. One of these crossed the channel at its narrowest point from what is still known as Grandique Ferry to Grandique Point. For some time, this was the chief link between Richmond County and Isle Madame. A new road to the ferry was built in 1829. Even though the ferry has long ceased to operate, it is still known as Grandique Ferry Road, while the community overlooking Lennox Passage is named Grandique Ferry.

Farther east, another ferry crossed the wider part of the channel between River Bourgeois and D'Escousse, a distance of three miles (five kilometres). The service was operated by a ferry operator on each side. In 1870, Peter Robinson, the ferry operator at River Bourgeois, was receiving a small sum from Richmond County, which had originally granted his licence. Stressing the danger and expense of running the ferry, he petitioned the assembly for provincial aid to put him on an equal footing with his counterpart at D'Escousse, who he had reason to believe received forty dollars annually from the government. The document has a large number of signatories, including Justices of the Peace and magistrates. We do not know the outcome, but it seems a reasonable request.

The third ferry site was where the bridge now crosses Lennox Passage. By 1844, the ferry there had become the main communication between Isle Madame and the mainland; however, embarking and disembarking were difficult because of the lack of proper ferry slips. An eloquent petition to the assembly, with many signatures, stated that this caused delays to passengers and mail, and the ferry operators were "exposed to much suffering and toil." They asked for one hundred pounds to build slips on either side, and for fifteen pounds for each of the ferry operators "for their extraordinary risk and labour in waiting upon and conveying mails and couriers throughout the year." Four years later, the complaints about the "insufficiency of the ferry" continued. Because of the lack of adequate wharves, there were still delays and difficulties in crossing with horses and carriages and in carrying the mail, produce, and purchases destined for Arichat. A request for funds for a team boat was referred, like so many others, to a committee. The journey was eventually made easier when wharves were built on either side of the channel.

The ferry was still running in 1886 when Senator Isidore LeBlanc, representing Richmond County, ran a spirited campaign for the construction of a drawbridge across Lennox Passage. His efforts were unsuccessful, and the

The Lennox Passage Bridge, ca 1922. Isle Madame was linked to the mainland of Cape Breton with the building of the Lennox Passage Bridge in 1919. This structure was replaced in the 1970s. [COURTESY ISLE MADAME HISTORICAL SOCIETY]

ferry was not replaced until 1919, with the opening of a swing bridge that was initially horse-powered, then mechanized. This in turn was finally replaced in 1970 by a causeway from the mainland to Burnt Island, continuing with a bascule, or movable, bridge to Isle Madame that allows vessels to pass through. The community on the mainland, formerly known as Lennox Ferry, is now called Lennox Passage.

For some years in the early twentieth century, a steam ferry connected Arichat to Canso, but it was discontinued in 1912.

BOULARDERIE ISLAND

Boularderie Island lies between Little and Big Bras d'Or, the channels that link the Atlantic Ocean to the tidal Bras d'Or Lake. The island, formerly known as Île de Verderonne, takes its present name from Louis-Simon le Poupet de la Boularderie who served at Louisbourg. In 1719, he was granted the island,

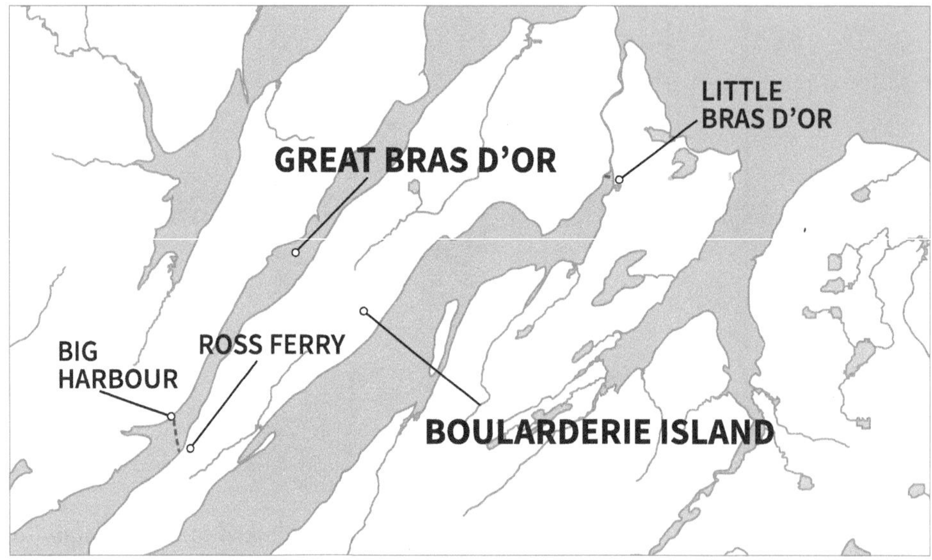

where he established a successful farm. The French left Île-Royale after the final fall of Louisbourg, and Boularderie Island remained uninhabited until the early nineteenth century, when Scottish settlers arrived in the newly named northern Cape Breton.

Just west of Great Bras d'Or, on St. Anns Harbour, a small group of French Jesuit missionaries came to the fortified settlement of Sainte-Anne in the 1630s. A few of them travelled overland to preach to the Mi'kmaq, who frequented the area that is now Baddeck. When the garrison at Sainte-Anne was transferred to Newfoundland in 1641, the Jesuit mission was withdrawn. The Mi'kmaq continued to frequent the area until the early nineteenth century, when Scottish settlers took up land along the Baddeck River. They cleared plots for farms, and their communities expanded to the surrounding area on the Bras d'Or Lake. Baddeck itself grew up in the 1820s, when merchant James Duffus established a business, first on Kidston Island, and then on the mainland. In 1851, Baddeck became the shire town of Victoria County.

The town of Sydney had been established on Spanish Bay since 1785. The Post Road from Sydney crossed the narrow channel of Little Bras d'Or to

Boularderie Island and the much wider Great Bras d'Or farther west. Travellers on the Post Road from Sydney to Baddeck crossed the narrow channel by boat, until a bridge was built over Little Bras d'Or in 1852. The original bridge did not last long: it was carried away by ice on December 2, 1854.

In January 1855, Patrick Howley established a ferry in its place. He used a boat and a scow to take passengers and their horses and buggies across the water. His service was much in demand; in January 1855 he petitioned the assembly for a grant to cover the cost of the boat and scow. He carried people who couldn't afford to pay in addition to his paying passengers, and his request was supported by many signatories. The ferry was later replaced by a swing bridge that served travellers for many years until the Trans-Canada Highway was established and the present bridge was constructed.

The Great Bras d'Or, nearly one mile (about one and a half kilometres) wide on average, was not bridged until 1961. Until then, a ferry linked the community of Ross Ferry with Big Harbour, carrying vehicles, passengers, and mail. This ferry was a vital connector for many years in the main road from Sydney to Baddeck, western Cape Breton Island, and mainland Nova Scotia.

John Ross and his wife Robina Mackenzie, immigrants from Scotland at the time of the Clearances, came to the west coast of Boularderie Island in 1821. Ross cleared land on Big Bras d'Or and received title to his two hundred acres (eighty-one hectares) in 1827. As well as farming his land, he operated a ferry on the island's western shore for the convenience of travellers. By 1851, John Ross had kept the ferry running from the island to Big Harbour for eighteen years, during which time traffic had increased. He had carried passengers, horses, and cattle, in all seasons, by day and night. Additionally, like other ferry operators he was required to transport the postman and his horse free of charge. He therefore petitioned the legislature for an increase in what he considered an inadequate allowance for his services, claiming that he had not received even that allowance in full and that he needed to purchase large enough boats and scows to accommodate the increased volume of traffic. His petition was endorsed by several residents, who observed that "the ferry kept by John Ross could not be dispensed with without great inconvenience to the

The Ross Ferry, operated by the Department of Highways, leaves from Big Harbour, NS, for the community of Ross Ferry on the opposite side of the Bras d'Or Lakes, ca. 1948. [NS ARCHIVES, NSIB NO. 3683]

publick." The ferry continued and was later operated by John's son Angus, who was assisted by Philip Fraser.

A boat based in Big Harbour on the mainland was run for many years by the Matheson family. By 1855, Kenneth Matheson was operating this ferry. For some time, he had received ten pounds a year for carrying the mail once a week. Now, the mail carrier crossed twice a week, which cost the ferry operator more money and time. Among his other passengers, many were too poor to pay the fare, so he carried them free of charge because, as he wrote in a petition to the assembly, "to refuse would subject him to a degree of unpopularity no person would willingly incur. The usage in this part of Cape Breton in matters of this kind, and in welcoming travellers for the night to entertainment and lodging without any charge, being so much a matter of course that no one would feel inclined to incur the odium of refusing either of these to travellers." On these grounds, and because of the additional cost of carrying the mail, he looked to the assembly for further subsidy.

The following year, John Ross also appealed for help. It seems that he was losing business to the steamer that provided a summer service between Sydney and Baddeck, leaving him to make the crossing in winter, contending with ice and bad weather. Not only did he have to carry the mail twice a week, but also his boat and scow had to accommodate men, horses, and cattle. His petition for a grant was backed by many signatories.

As in other communities around Nova Scotia, these ferry services were originally a sideline from farming, and they ran on demand for about one hundred years. As time went on, it became clear that on such an important route a regular, dedicated service was necessary. In the mid-1920s, the provincial Department of Highways took over, and government employees carried out the operation. Jess Matheson of Big Harbour was among the last private ferry operators.

With the government service, rowboats and scows were replaced by steamers. Buggies were outnumbered by cars, and gradually, larger, more modern vessels were brought into service. By the 1930s, the car-carrying ferry was capable of keeping a path open through the ice under most conditions.

After the Second World War, the volume of traffic serving residents and tourists increased, and by 1950, it was clear from the lineups of cars that the ferry across Great Bras d'Or Channel was inadequate to meet the demand. A new vessel was built in 1959, carrying ten cars and one hundred passengers, but this was still insufficient. Planning had begun for what would become known as the Seal Island Bridge, which was opened in 1961. The ferry boats were discontinued and the employees dismissed, but the small community on Boularderie Island is still known as Ross Ferry. Many of the former ferry employees moved away in search of work, with a consequent drop in the populations of Big Cove and Ross Ferry.

FERRIES AROUND THE MINAS BASIN AND THE BRAS D'OR LAKES

The largest bodies of water within Nova Scotia are the Minas Basin, sheltered by the Blomidon Peninsula at the head of the Bay of Fundy, and the Bras d'Or Lakes in Cape Breton, which consist of a broad tidal estuary system with two channels feeding into the Atlantic Ocean. Mi'kmaw canoes first navigated these watercourses that constituted major travel routes for their semi-nomadic culture.

From about 1700, Acadians diked marshlands around the Minas Basin to create productive farmland and establish communities. The largest of these was Grand Pré, on the southern shore of the basin. Other Acadian communities grew up on the rivers flowing into the basin and along its northern shore. In 1755, the Acadians were driven into exile by the British. Five years later, Governor Charles Lawrence invited New Englanders to take over the abandoned farmlands to bring them back into production. New townships were created, and communities of Planters replaced the Acadian villages. These newer settlers made their living by fishing and farming.

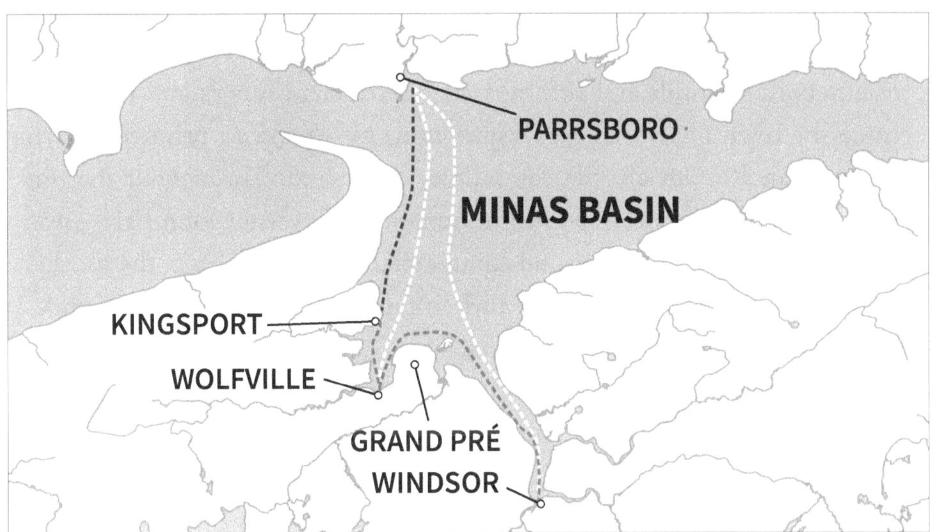

MINAS BASIN

Situated on the northern shore of the Minas Channel opposite Cape Blomidon, Partridge Island is treasured by the Mi'kmaq, for whom it holds important connections with the legendary Kluskap, teacher and creator central to the Mi'kmaw culture. The island also offered an ample source of stone for tools and weapons. Across the water, Blomidon, too, featured in stories of Kluskap. These sites, sacred to the Mi'kmaq, were disregarded by colonists as they claimed these areas for their own.

When the Acadians formed communities around the Minas Basin, they relied on the trail from the Minas Basin through the Cobequid Mountains to communicate with their neighbours in the Acadian village of Beaubassin on the Cumberland Basin. This trail was later used by British settlers, two of whom received land in the 1770s on the shore behind Partridge Island, at the mouth of Farrells River.

Among the others who joined the growing British population was James Ratchford, who came in 1779 to Partridge Island, as the settlement on the shore was also known. Ratchford soon dominated the community with his commercial undertakings. He opened a store and a hotel, and he established a lumber mill and shipyard on the western shore of Farrells River. Other entrepreneurs built sawmills and shipyards as a settlement was established, which became the town of Parrsboro. Despite raids by American privateers during the American Revolution, the community prospered. Throughout the nineteenth century, Parrsboro—named in honour of Governor John Parr—was a thriving centre of shipbuilding and commercial shipping. It lay at the southern end of the trail across the Cobequid Mountains, where a road (now Trunk 2) was built leading northwest to Amherst.

The Parrsboro area was the site of one of the province's oldest ferry services. Before the Expulsion, the Acadians on the northern shore of the Minas Basin needed a means of staying in touch with their friends on the far side. From about 1730 until the mid-1750s, Jean Bourg and François Arseneau operated a ferry from the mouth of Farrells River to the farming communities on the basin's southern shore.

The handful of British settlers who came later to the Partridge Island area also needed to travel to communities across the water. Three men were offered free land in return for agreeing to run a ferry, replacing the Acadian ferry, which would serve Partridge Island Harbour and Windsor—at that time the chief town on the southern shore of the basin. The Minas Basin was in a vulnerable location. During the American Revolution, Abijah Scott's ferry, a sailboat, was attacked twice by privateers. After the first attempt, it was quickly recovered. The second time it wasn't so lucky, and the raiders destroyed the boat. Peace that followed the revolution allowed for the reinstatement of the ferry, but the service was irregular in the nineteenth century.

By 1842, James Ratchford, the most influential businessman of Partridge Island, had added the Minas Basin ferry service to his other interests. Passengers, however, found the ferry unsatisfactory. They complained in a petition to the legislative assembly that service was erratic; the crew, frequently drunk, paid no attention to the comfort of the passengers; and no meals were available on board. They asked that the ferry subsidy should be extended to "Messrs. Cochrane of Windsor," who would provide a more suitable vessel. The Cochranes' service was also irregular from time to time, but this was usually due to "causes beyond [the proprietors'] control," when heavy seas would make it unsafe to carry horses and carriages or cattle. It was also hard to find a sober crew. The previous captain of Cochrane's ferry had been a member of the Temperance Society; the current one, apparently, was not. The petitioners sought an increased subsidy for improved accommodation. A war of petitions and counter-petitions continued. At one point, Ratchford claimed he had run a ferry for forty years from Partridge Island to Windsor and Horton, from April until Christmas, often beginning earlier and ending later.

Improvements to the ferry service were in the wind in 1843, when sail gave way to steam. A packet serving Horton, Parrsboro, and Windsor was built at great expense with the expectation that it would receive a sufficient subsidy to make it viable. It had to be abandoned after only two seasons because it was unprofitable. By 1848, the *Ruth and Hannah* was serving Horton, Parrsboro, and Windsor. The *Ruth and Hannah* was much larger than a previous ferry, *Tom Pringle*, but apparently it was still inadequate for travellers' needs. The following year, a petition signed by many residents asked for provincial assistance for a larger vessel to carry the increased seasonal traffic as well as the mail.

In the nineteenth century, the chief towns on the Minas Basin were Parrsboro on the northern shore; Windsor at the mouth of the Avon River (formerly the Acadian village of Pisiquid); Horton at the mouth of the Gaspereau River, just east of Grand Pré; and Kingsport to the west. Many residents of Horton moved along the shore to form the community of Wolfville, originally known as Mud Creek.

Lying at the mouth of the Avon River that flows into the Minas Basin from the south, Windsor grew up around Fort Edward, built in 1750, which still dominates the town. Prominent Halifax citizens bought land in Windsor to develop businesses or to serve as retreats from the busy life of the capital. The community was linked to Halifax by a road that became Nova Scotia's first stagecoach route. Shipbuilding and merchant shipping became the chief sources of Windsor's prosperity.

Wolfville, farther west, was the social, commercial, and administrative centre for Horton Township. Its small harbour supported trading vessels and was

Ferry Evangeline *heading out of Digby Gap, NS.* [NS ARCHIVES, W. R. MACASKILL 1987-453 NUMBER 1047]

surrounded by shipyards, commercial wharves, and merchants' warehouses for many years. But the larger steamships that replaced trading schooners from the mid-1800s could not access the harbour. A rail line was built across it in 1868, putting an end to Wolfville's merchant shipping. Acadia University, which was established in 1838, stimulated the town's economic growth. Today Wolfville welcomes tourists to its nearby farm markets and wineries.

Kingsport, on the western shore of the Minas Basin, lies south of Blomidon between the Pereaux and the Habitant Rivers, in what was formerly the Acadian parish of St. Joseph des Mines. Following the Acadian Expulsion, New Englanders came to what was established in 1760 as Cornwallis Township. A farming and major shipbuilding centre, it was an important port on the Minas Basin. Many large ships were built here, and by the end of the nineteenth century it was served by the Cornwallis Valley Railway. In 1891, special trains were added to bring visitors to Kingsport to view the launch of *Canada,* one of the largest full-rigged ships ever built in this country. Today, sawmills and shipyards have gone, and Kingsport is a quiet rural village.

The MV Kipawo *leaving Parrsboro, NS.* [NS ARCHIVES]

With the opening of the Windsor and Annapolis Railway in 1869, the mail was transported by a circuitous land route, and the ferry no longer called at Windsor, leaving former passengers without a ferry. A petition with many signatories from Kings and Hants Counties supported the offer of Captain James Eagles to take over the Windsor ferry service, but nothing more was heard of it.

The other residents around the Minas Basin still had their ferry. For most of the nineteenth century and well into the twentieth, a daily service ran between Parrsboro, Kingsport, and Wolfville, using first sailboats and later steamers. From 1893 until 1904, the *Evangeline* worked the triangular route, followed by the *Prince Albert,* which served until 1926. In that year, the MV *Kipawo,* a steel vessel built in the shipyard at Saint John for the Dominion Atlantic Railway, took over for transport on the Minas Basin. The vessel, taking its name from the three ports it served, carried cars, which were loaded by crane. The ferry ran until 1942, when in the Second World War it became part of Canada's naval defence system, and the ferry service was terminated. From this time onward, travel around the Minas Basin was by land.

After the war, MV *Kipawo* was abandoned in Newfoundland. In 1982, a group dedicated to preserving it brought it back to Parrsboro. Here the vessel has been repurposed as a cultural and performance centre and the base for the Ship's Company Theatre, which holds plays and concerts every summer.

COBEQUID BAY

Cobequid Bay lies at the eastern end of the Minas Basin. There are many small communities on each side of the bay, some of them dating back to the early eighteenth century when Acadians came to the area. On the south side, the village of Noel was named for Noël Doiron, who settled there with his family in 1710 and remained until 1750, when they moved to Île Saint-Jean. The village lay abandoned until the 1770s, when Ulster Scots came from the New England colonies to resettle the area. They established shipyards, including one operated by the O'Brien family from which twenty vessels were launched. Among them were *Amanda,* the largest, and the barque *Noel.* Jutting out into the bay to the west is Burntcoat Head, where the world's greatest tidal range occurs.

East from Noel, the community of Douglas was situated on the west side of the Shubenacadie estuary, where the long, meandering Shubenacadie River flows into Cobequid Bay. Douglas was the administrative centre of the Township of Douglas, established in the 1760s to receive Planters from the New England colonies. Maitland, as Douglas would eventually be known, became the most prominent shipbuilding community along the shore. It was not only home to at least four shipyards, the first of which was owned by the family of David Whidden, one of the earliest settlers, but the community also served as the western terminus for ferries across the Shubenacadie River. The town's most famous vessel, the *William D. Lawrence,* was launched from the Lawrence family shipyard in 1874.

On the northern side of Cobequid Bay, the area around Debert is one of the earliest known sites of Indigenous habitation, dating back nearly ten thousand years. Today, small farming communities like Great Village lie along the bay's shore and river valleys. The area that is now Great Village became home to Acadian settlers in the 1630s. They diked marshes to create farmland in

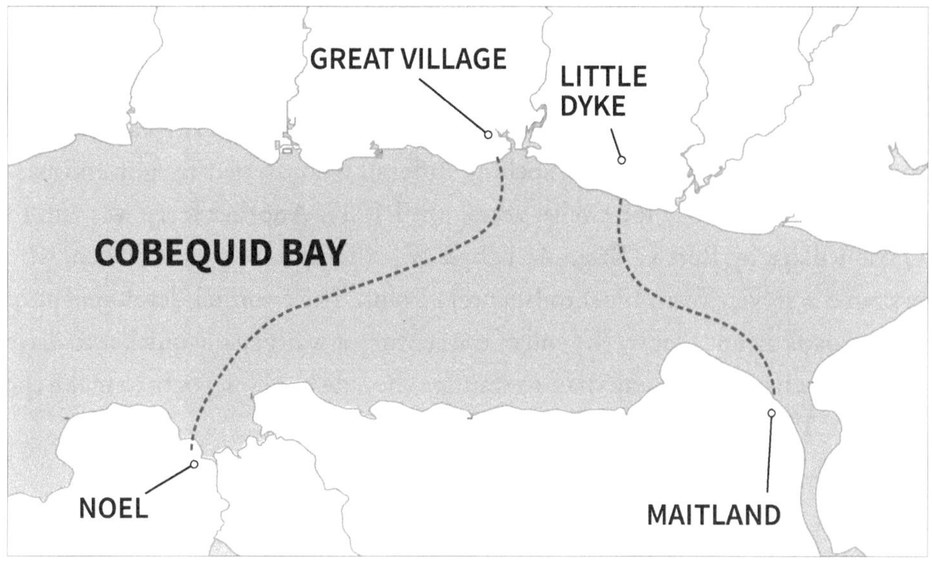

the place they called Petit Louis or Vil de Cadets. A *cadet* is a younger son or brother, suggesting that the settlers were younger members of families whose older offspring farmed elsewhere.

After the British forced the Acadians into exile, the Township of Londonderry was created to receive Protestant settlers. Families from New England colonies, most originally from Ulster, came in the 1760s to take over the abandoned Acadian farms in the township. They made their living by the typical farming, fishing, sawmilling, and shipbuilding.

Communication with the communities on the other side of the bay was achieved by boat, or by way of Truro at the head of the bay. In the mid-nineteenth century, there were several ferries across Cobequid Bay. They were dependent on the tides; because of the extensive mud flats at low tide, boats could come to shore only at high water. Elinor Maher, in her book *Cobequid Bay Ferries*, describes the traffic across the bay from 1854. In that year, Isaiah Smith, who was born in Kennetcook, ran a ferry from Douglas to Londonderry Township, probably landing at Little Dyke, near Glenholme on the opposite side. By the following year, the ferry was run by a Mrs. Smith, presumably Isaiah's wife, Lydia.

In 1866, William Stewart of Londonderry ran the ferry from Maitland to Little Dyke. His small sailboats ran daily, except for Sunday, at high tide when the water was deep enough for them approach the shore. The same route was served in the early twentieth century by Alexander Stuart (perhaps from the same family, although the spelling differs), who carried freight and passengers across the bay for twelve years, until 1925. Another ferry was run to Great Village by Bert O'Brien on behalf of his father, Johnson O'Brien, who operated a service from Noel to Spencers Point. The eventual development of better roads meant that by the end of the century it was usually quicker to drive around the head of the bay than to wait for the tide to allow boats to make the crossing. Thus, these ferries ceased to operate.

THE BRAS D'OR LAKES

The Bras d'Or Lakes, which occupy the central part of Cape Breton Island, consist of a large body of water fed by numerous rivers, with outlets to the Atlantic Ocean on either side of Boularderie Island.

The ferry dock and church at Little Narrows. [NS ARCHIVES, CLARA DENNIS 1981-541 NUMBER 656CB]

LITTLE NARROWS

On the western side of the Iona Peninsula, where St. Patricks Channel narrows, only a short distance separates the peninsula from the land on the opposite side. A cable-operated ferry provides a link from the small road leading off Highway 105 to the village of Little Narrows on the Iona Peninsula, which was settled by Scottish immigrants in the early nineteenth century.

Known as a source of gypsum for many years, Little Narrows, like its neighbours at Iona and Grand Narrows, was formerly a community of small farmers. They rowed across the narrow strait, and ferried travellers along the road toward Iona and the Grand Narrows ferry on the eastern side of the Iona Peninsula. In 1989, the Little Narrows ferry was listed among those operated by the provincial government. Today's cable ferry remains a provincial responsibility.

GRAND NARROWS

In 1800, four McNeils from the island of Barra in the Outer Hebrides settled on the western side of Barra Strait, on the Washabuck Peninsula in the Bras d'Or Lake, initiating the community now known as Grand Narrows. Shortly after their arrival, Hector McNeil, also from Barra, came to settle on the peninsula, on the opposite side of the Barra Strait. McNeil was joined by other emigrants from Barra, many of them also McNeils. They cleared land for farming, cut lumber, and fished in the Bras d'Or Lake. They named their community Iona, after the Scottish island. These settlers were all Gaelic-speaking Roman Catholics, many of them part of extended families, and residents often rowed across the strait to visit friends and relatives.

In 1847, a locally operated ferry service was initiated to serve the two communities. Travellers between the Canso Strait and northern Cape Breton also used this ferry. After the opening of a railway bridge across the strait in 1890, some of these travellers opted for the train. Road traffic continued to rely on the ferry, which was taken over by the provincial government by 1989. The ferry service was superseded by a road bridge that was completed four years later, and the ferry ceased operations. In 2022, the old ferry wharf, still found at Grand Narrows, was recognized as a heritage site by the Cape Breton Regional Municipality.

5

Interprovincial Ferries: Atlantic Canada and Quebec

The Northumberland Strait, with its renowned warm waters, separates the provinces of Nova Scotia and Prince Edward Island. Before the completion of the Confederation Bridge in 1996, communication and travel between the neighbouring provinces was of necessity by water. In the case of Nova Scotia's connection with New Brunswick, a land route served the eastern part of both provinces, but for western areas, the journey could be shortened by a ferry across the Bay of Fundy. At one time, a ferry from Pictou to the Magdalen Islands even provided a link to Quebec. Ferries continue to cross the waters between these provinces today, though one of the original routes to Prince Edward Island has been replaced by the eight-mile (thirteen-kilometre) Confederation Bridge. The ferry to the Magdalen Islands now departs from Souris, at the eastern end of Prince Edward Island; the crossing takes about five hours. One of the longest routes among the year-round interprovincial ferry services, ranging between six and eight hours, exists between North Sydney, NS, and Port aux Basques, NL. There is also a more recent seasonal ferry service, established in 1967, that runs between North Sydney and Argentia, NL, which is longer still at about fifteen hours, although this one does not operate daily.

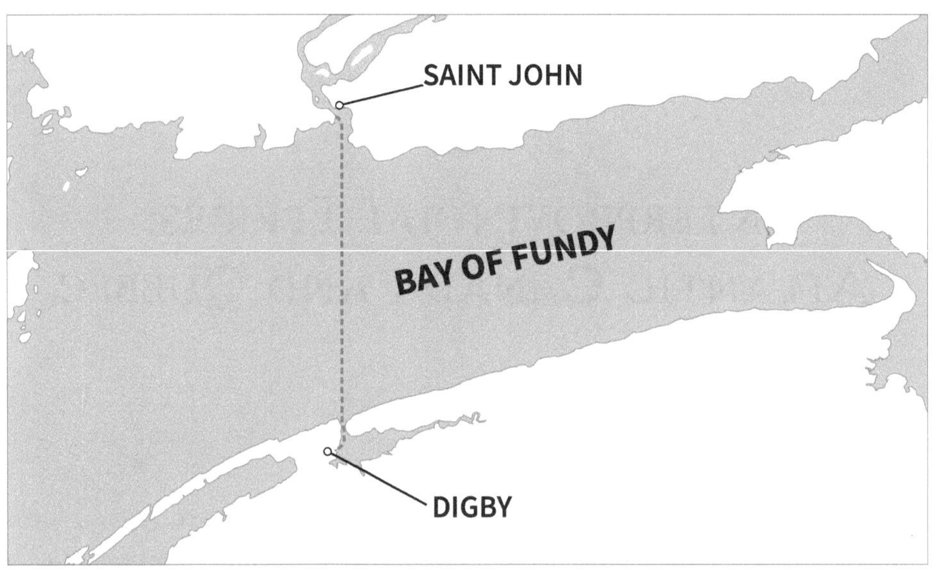

NOVA SCOTIA TO NEW BRUNSWICK

Nova Scotia's mainland border with New Brunswick lies at the head of the Bay of Fundy on Chignecto Bay, where the Missaguash River flows across the Chignecto Isthmus, a few kilometres north of Amherst. It is more than 120 miles (200 kilometres) from this border to Saint John, New Brunswick's commercial centre. Digby, NS, is a similar distance from the same border, and lies directly south of Saint John, across the Bay of Fundy. Travel across the bay is a much more direct route for residents of western Nova Scotia and New Brunswick than the land route between the two provinces.

Digby, at the western end of the Annapolis Basin, was first known as Oositookun (ear of land) to the Mi'kmaq, who first travelled from there by canoe across the basin to the Annapolis River. In 1604, the French explorers led by Pierre Dugua de Monts sailed through nearby Digby Gut, as we know it today, and first glimpsed the basin that they called Port-Royal. The following year, an expedition returned to build a small, fortified settlement known today as the Port-Royal Habitation. The Habitation structure was short-lived due to a British raid. In 1636, a new contingent of French colonists was transferred from LaHave to the mouth of what is now the Annapolis River to form the community of Port-Royal, which served as the capital of Acadie for many years. Its residents formed the nucleus of what would flourish to become the Acadian population.

Following the Acadian Expulsion by the British that commenced in 1755, Port-Royal became Annapolis Royal, and settlers were brought from the New England colonies. In the 1780s, Loyalist refugees fleeing the aftermath of the American Revolution received grants of land near the entrance to the Annapolis Basin, where the town and township of Digby were established. Digby took its name from a distinguished admiral of the British Royal Navy, and the narrow entrance from the Bay of Fundy became known as Digby Gut. The settlers of Digby eventually prospered, making a living by fishing, shipbuilding, and merchant shipping at this strategic location.

Across the bay, Saint John lies in the ancestral territory of the Mi'kmaq and the Wolastoqiyik (or Maliseet), where the Saint John River they called Wolastoq (beautiful river) was an important route to the St. Lawrence. When de Monts and Samuel de Champlain arrived at the estuary on June 24, 1604, which is recognized as the feast day of Saint John the Baptist, they named the river and harbour Saint Jean.

In 1631, Charles de Saint-Étienne de La Tour built a fort on the east side of this river's mouth for the purpose of trading. La Tour was forced from his settlement in the Cape Sable area in the early 1640s by his rival for power in Acadie, Charles de Menou d'Aulnay, and retreated to his base at Saint John. In 1645, the fort was stormed by d'Aulnay's forces, while La Tour was away seeking support in Boston. Although the fort was bravely defended by La Tour's wife and his men, it fell to the attackers. A small Acadian community remained at the river mouth until the Expulsion of 1755.

During the American Revolution, Saint John was attacked and briefly occupied by American forces, but they did not remain. A wave of Loyalists arrived in 1783 and quickly set up homes and businesses there. Pressure from settlers to the area resulted in the construction of Fort Howe in 1777 to help defend them against further attack from American privateers. In 1785, Saint

John was the first to receive a royal charter incorporating it as a city. The blockhouse of Fort Howe is recognized today as a National Historic Site.

Merchants flourished in the nineteenth century, and an important shipbuilding industry developed. Trading vessels sailed on a triangular route between Saint John, the Caribbean, and Britain. The population grew quickly with an influx of Irish immigrants, which contributed to a period of great prosperity. The city's wealth declined with iron steamers supplanting the wooden sailing ships, although Saint John remains the commercial centre of the region. Today, its major industry is oil refining.

Vessels from the Digby, NS, wharf have crossed the Bay of Fundy between the two provinces for many years. In early days, merchant shipping schooners might carry travellers across to avoid the long journey by land, but in the nineteenth century people felt the need for a more formal service. R. Baden Powell's article "The Bay of Fundy Ferry," in the *Nova Scotia Historical Quarterly* 2, no. 3 (1972), describes the complex history of the vessels that served this route. The earliest regular ferry named the *St. John*, a paddleboat equipped with sails, was owned by John Ward, Richard Smith, Hugh Johnston, and Peter Fraser. It began service on the Bay of Fundy crossing in 1827. In 1828, the ship ran from Saint John to Digby and Annapolis Royal, and the following year the operators received a subsidy of £50. Shortly afterward, it was bought by James Whitney. The ferry carried the mail, for which the operator received a payment of £150 in 1830.

James Whitney later received a grant for a larger vessel. In 1834, he operated what he called his "very superior vessel" *Henrietta*, from Windsor, NS, to Saint John, NB, then Saint Andrews, NB, and Eastport, ME. The ship had a fifty horsepower engine and featured comfortable accommodation for the lengthy journey. But like so many ferries, its cost of operation exceeded the income it produced. Whitney asked for assistance, without which he could not afford to serve the town of Windsor. The response was not recorded, but a second vessel, *Maid of the Mist*, was brought into service.

Whitney continued to operate the Fundy crossing with a series of steamers. This service seems to have been deemed inadequate by 1852, when a petition

The Prince Rupert *on September 16, 1909. This ship was in service between 1895 and 1913. It was the first on this service designed to make train connections.* [NS ARCHIVES, ADMIRAL DIGBY MUSEUM P12683]

with many signatures was received by the legislature for a steam ferry from Nova Scotia to New Brunswick. This vessel would carry cattle and sheep for market in Saint John, as well as produce and passengers. The carriage of freight remains a significant part of the service today between Digby and Saint John.

The King brothers took over the Fundy service in 1885, running from Windsor to Annapolis to Digby and then Saint John. The Nova Scotia Steamship Company's *Secret* began operating on the route at the same time, and ran until 1888, when the crossings became irregular. A federal vessel was brought in to provide more reliable service for that season.

The assembly received an unusual request in 1856. For many years, Edward Leonard of Digby had been raising a signal announcing the arrival and departure of the ferry carrying Her Majesty's mail. He now—perhaps with prompting from friends or family—asked for remuneration for his services and was allotted five pounds.

The Princess Helene *was in service between Digby, NS, and Saint John, NB, from 1930 and 1963.* [NS ARCHIVES, ADMIRAL DIGBY MUSEUM P15259]

A paddle-wheel steamer named *City of Monticello,* owned by the Bay of Fundy Steamship Company, began operations in 1889 with three crossings each week from Annapolis to Saint John. Two years later, the railway from Halifax was extended to Digby, which replaced Annapolis as the ferry terminal. When the Dominion Atlantic Railway was formed in 1894, the company took over the ferry service, adding the *Prince Rupert.* At Digby, rail passengers for New Brunswick and the United States transferred to a paddle-wheel steamship that was replaced in 1903 by the propeller-driven SS *Yarmouth.*

The ferries brought freight and passengers to Nova Scotia from beyond New Brunswick as well, including tourists from Boston, MA, and Central Canada. Among the vessels serving the route was the *Princess Helene,* which ran for thirty-three years before being retired in 1963. It was the first passenger-car ferry to make the crossing. *Princess of Acadia* took over the service with a significantly increased capacity: up to 1,000 passengers, 120 cars, and railcar freight. The steamship was replaced in 1971 with a diesel engine ship of the same name, which featured a reduced passenger capacity but an increased vehicle capacity.

Today, the Bay Ferries vessel MV *Fundy Rose* carries vehicles and passengers across the Bay of Fundy in just over two hours. The service is supported by both provincial governments. The emphasis on commercial traffic has been maintained to this day, with refrigerated trucks carrying lobsters, an important export from southwestern Nova Scotia, on the first stage of their journey to the United States.

NOVA SCOTIA TO PRINCE EDWARD ISLAND

The first French colonists on Île Saint-Jean formed a small community in the 1720s around Port-LaJoye, first known as Skmaqn by the Indigenous population, now Charlottetown Harbour, and on the neighbouring river, now known as the Hillsborough. Port-LaJoye was built to protect the harbour. (Today it is known as Skmaqn–Port-la-Joye–Fort Amherst National Historic Site, a testament to the four cultures associated with the location.) French settlement expanded to St. Peters Bay and a few other coastal communities, where the residents made their living by fishing and subsistence farming. In the mid-eighteenth century, when tension between the British and Acadians was mounting, some Acadians took the opportunity to leave Nova Scotia and escape to Île Saint-Jean. Their fears were confirmed in 1755 as they learned of the mass enforced exile in Nova Scotia.

After Quebec fell to British forces in 1759, France would soon lose the last of its colonies in the Maritimes by the 1763 Treaty of Paris. Île Saint-Jean became St. John's Island, and in 1799 it was renamed Prince Edward Island in honour of the Duke of Kent. When the British took control of the island, the majority of Acadians were deported from there as well. Some, however,

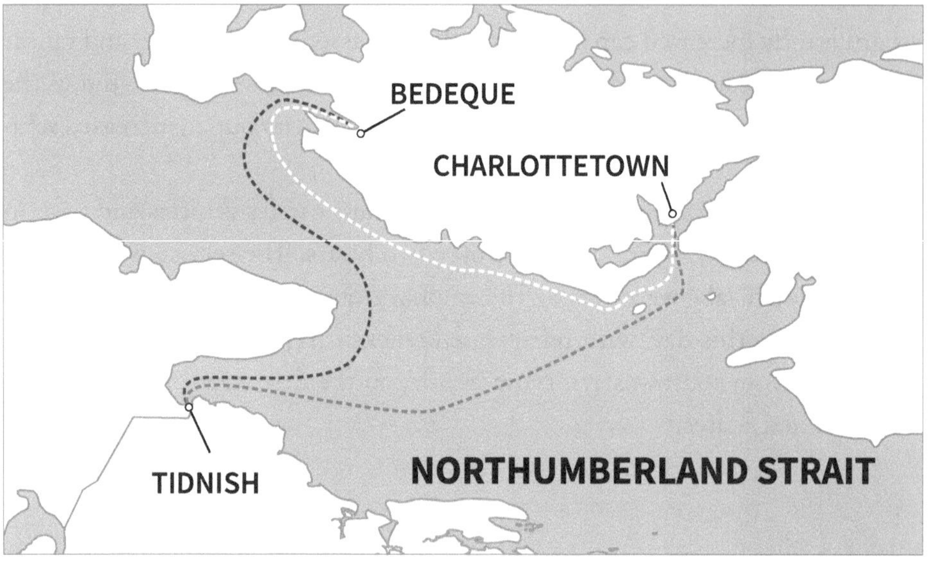

remained; there is still a small Acadian population on Prince Edward Island. The island's capital was established in 1768 at Charlottetown, the former site of Port-LaJoye. Fort Amherst initially replaced the French fort, but was later abandoned in favour of Charlottetown's Fort Edward, across the harbour.

On the Nova Scotia mainland side of the Northumberland Strait, the earliest British settlers came to Pictou from the Philadelphia area in the 1760s, followed by nearly one hundred Scots who arrived on the *Hector* in 1773 to settle along the shore and rivers. They made their living by forestry, farming, and fishing. The 1800s saw the development of coal mining in the inland area on the East River and the subsequent development of the major industrial areas of New Glasgow and Stellarton. Elsewhere along the Northumberland shore, communities around the harbours developed fishing and forestry industries.

At the eastern end of the border between Nova Scotia and New Brunswick, the deep bay known as Baie Verte was a haven for European fishing vessels from the seventeenth century. The Tidnish River flows into the south side of the bay, in Nova Scotia. Here, the promontory of Tidnish Head shelters the harbour. Tidnish, now the site of a Nova Scotian provincial park, lies a little to the east of the estuary.

The forms of transportation to navigate the Northumberland Strait changed over time. At first, the Mi'kmaq paddled sturdy sea canoes across the strait. When European settlers came to the area, they relied on their fishing boats to carry them across, but in the early eighteenth century, years of enmity discouraged travel between the English and the French colonies. In the 1740s, when many Acadians decided to seek a safe haven in Île Saint-Jean to escape British rule, fishing boats transported them and their belongings across the narrowest part of the strait to Port-LaJoye.

Once the British had control of the island, travel from the mainland became easier, but it would still be some time before a formal seasonal ferry was established. It ran from in Nova Scotia to points on the island, by the shortest crossing on the Northumberland Strait. In the summer of 1840, William Weeks of Tidnish began providing a fortnightly service with his schooner *Christy* from Baie Verte to the island's communities of Bedeque and Charlottetown. Early in 1841, he planned to offer this service again the following summer, but he needed "reasonable encouragement" from the assembly because the profits from the service did not meet his expenses. His petition was countersigned by several Justices of the Peace and MLAs. He received twenty pounds, but by the next year he still could not make ends meet and asked for a further increase.

In 1843, after running the ferry for three seasons, Weeks was planning to replace the *Christy* with "a superior vessel" for which he requested a grant from the assembly. A testimonial from his many supporters stated that Weeks was a young man of industrious habits who had demonstrated indefatigable assiduity in operating the ferry. His petition, like many at this time, was referred to the Committee on Navigation Securities. Whether or not his request was granted, he continued to run the ferry. The following year, he planned to continue the fortnightly service, calling at Bedeque and Charlottetown alternately, and again applied for assistance, backed by Bell Chappell, a local Justice of the Peace. His petition was evidently tabled, but the outcome is not recorded.

In 1849, Marcus Chappell was planning his summer activities. He would sail his schooner *Dorothy* weekly from Baie Verte to Bedeque and Charlottetown alternately for the busy three months' summer season, and then cut the service

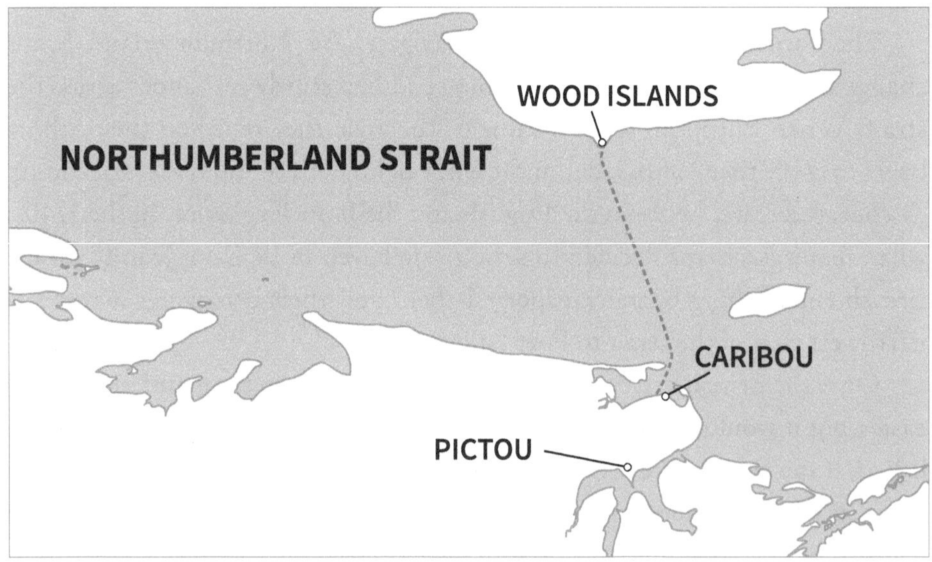

to once every two weeks in the fall. He calculated that charging a reasonable rate would not bring him sufficient profit and sought a subsidy. Again, the response is unknown, but the service seems to have continued.

The development of postal services brought about changes and caused some rivalry between ferry operators who vied for the government contract to transport mail. By the mid-1850s, ferries were carrying both mail and passengers from Nova Scotia to ports on Prince Edward Island. In 1855, the steamer *Rosebud,* built the previous year by William Heard of Charlottetown, left from Baie Verte and called at Charlottetown and Pictou, with a contract to transport the mail. The mail contract was later given to the *Lady LeMarchant.* Although Heard lost the grant for mail, the *Rosebud* continued to carry passengers, freight, and livestock. Early in 1856, Heard applied for a renewal of his subsidy, claiming to offer better service than his rival. He received two hundred pounds, and his ferry service continued.

Also in the mid-1850s, William Chappell was providing a weekly ferry service from Baie Verte to Charlottetown with his schooner *Wm. Nelson.* He stated in a petition to the assembly that he was building a "more commodious" schooner that he hoped to put into service the following spring, with

Northumberland Ferries' MV Confederation *traveling from Caribou, NS, to Wood Islands, PEI, in 2015.* [TONY WEBSTER VIA WIKIMEDIA COMMONS]

accommodation for "lady passengers." Chappell received a grant of twenty-five pounds. The Baie Verte area continued for many years to be the point of departure for ferries to Prince Edward Island. The western terminal shifted across the border to New Brunswick. The Confederation Bridge, which opened to traffic in 1997, replaced the ferry.

A second ferry service, from Caribou, NS, to Wood Islands, PEI, is operated by Northumberland Ferries Limited's subsidiary Bay Ferries, with a subsidy from the federal government. It has run in spring, summer, and fall since 1941, when the first vessel, *Prince Nova,* came into service. It carried cars and trucks as well as passengers until 1958. *Charles A. Dunning* joined the service in 1946 and operated until it was replaced in 1963 by a new car-carrying ferry, a second *Prince Nova,* which ran until 1997. *Lord Selkirk* joined the fleet in 1958 and served until 1993. Since then, two vessels have been in service. *Prince Edward* operated from 1972 to 1997, when it was replaced by *Holiday Island. Confederation* joined it in 1975 and served until 1993.

In recent years, this route has been beset by problems. In July 2022 a fire on *Holiday Island* took it out of service. It was replaced by MV *Saaremaa,* on loan from Quebec. The service has continued but has once experienced numerous disruptions.

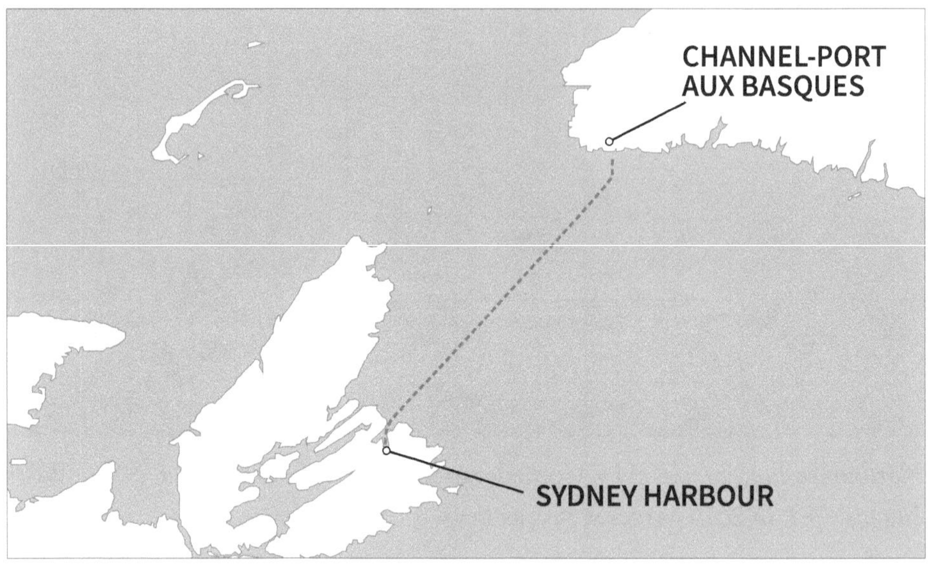

NOVA SCOTIA TO NEWFOUNDLAND AND LABRADOR

The island of Newfoundland was the once the exclusive territory of the Beothuk and Mi'kmaq, and it was one of the earliest areas of North America to be accessed by European explorers. Norsemen from Iceland and Greenland founded a short-lived settlement at L'Anse aux Meadows in about 1000 AD. In the late fifteenth century, fishing boats from several European countries began to work seasonally on the offshore banks. Cod was plentiful, and the fish were salted on board, to be dried upon return to Europe. Meanwhile, British fishing boats concentrated on waters closer to the shore, drying their catch on land before returning home.

In 1583, Sir Humphrey Gilbert claimed Newfoundland for England, but French fishing vessels also frequented the island's harbours, where they established seasonal fishing bases. In the seventeenth century, both countries built year-round coastal fishing settlements, where French and English place names endure today. The two nations vied for control of the island for many years. The 1713 Treaty of Utrecht decisively awarded Newfoundland to the British, with provision for seasonal French fishing. French names for harbours all around the coast remind us of the island's long and complicated history. Newfoundland officially became a British Crown colony in 1825, with its capital at St. John's.

During the latter years of the Second World War, an American air base brought prosperity to St. John's, but the outports were still struggling for survival, and by the mid-twentieth century the colony's economy had deteriorated. In 1948, Newfoundlanders voted to join Canada, and the following year the island along with the Labrador territory became its tenth province (although its name would not become Newfoundland and Labrador until 2001). Between 1954 and 1975 many of the outports were closed down, and their residents were resettled in larger communities.

NORTH SYDNEY TO PORT AUX BASQUES

The community of Port aux Basques is situated in southwestern Newfoundland and is officially known as Channel-Port aux Basques. The name evokes the 1500s, when fishers from the Basque Country, a cultural region of southwestern France, crossed the Atlantic Ocean annually to catch cod and shelter their vessels in the ice-free harbour.

Although the harbour was used by European fishing boats, a colonial settlement did not grow up until the early 1700s, when fishers from the Channel Islands established a land base that they called Channel. Other French and English fishing settlements grew up at that time, including the nearby village of Port aux Basques, which is the name recorded by Captain James Cook in a survey made in the 1760s. Port aux Basques remained a fishing village until 1857, when a telegraph station was opened there. Forty years later, it became the terminus of the Newfoundland Railway, and a new era of history began.

Port aux Basques is the place in the province of Newfoundland and Labrador nearest to Cape Breton, and therefore an ideal location for communication between Nova Scotia and Newfoundland. The ferry linking the provinces dates back to the late nineteenth century. It was made possible by the companies that operated railways in both jurisdictions. The 1880s saw the beginning of the construction of the narrow-gauge Newfoundland Northern

The Marine Atlantic ferry Blue Puttees, *August 2011.* [HAYDN BLACKEY, VIA WIKIMEDIA COMMONS]

and Western Railway linking St. John's with other communities in the colony. It took many years to build its circuitous route, and the original construction company declared bankruptcy in 1884. The final section to Port aux Basques was completed only in 1898.

On the Nova Scotia side, shipbuilding and merchant shipping had developed in the town of North Sydney in the early nineteenth century. Wooden shipbuilding declined toward the end of the century, but the economy was sustained by steam-powered trading vessels that linked the harbour with ports around the world. When a section of the Intercolonial Railway line came to North Sydney from New Glasgow in 1890, it would add a new dimension to the town's economy. With the opening of the Newfoundland Railway to Port aux Basques in 1898, the time had come for a passenger ferry between the two ports. The Reid Newfoundland Company's first ferry left Port aux Basques for

North Sydney on July 1, 1898. The Reid railway company and its ferry service were taken over by the Newfoundland government in 1923.

The government-operated Newfoundland Railway continued to operate the ferry. A new vessel, *Caribou,* came into service in 1925. In October 1942 tragedy struck. *Caribou* was en route from North Sydney to Port aux Basques when a German submarine patrolling the Newfoundland coast torpedoed the ferry; 136 lives were lost.

When Newfoundland formally joined the Canadian confederation in 1949, Canadian National Railway took over the Newfoundland Railway company and its ferry service. The last passenger train to Port aux Basques ran in 1969. Today travellers from St. John's have to drive the long route across the island on the Trans-Canada Highway to reach the ferry. The company continued to operate as CN Marine until 1986, when ferries in the Atlantic provinces were taken over by Marine Atlantic. A second *Caribou* and a new vessel, *Joseph and Clara Smallwood,* came into service. Their successors, *Highlanders* and *Blue Puttees,* have been in operation since 2011.

Ferry passengers from the 1890s would not recognize today's vessels travelling between the provinces of Nova Scotia and Newfoundland and Labrador. There are restaurants, bars, and movie theatres on the ferries, and sleeping accommodation is also available for passengers. The crossing takes around seven hours, with several sailings every day, depending on the season and the weather. In 1967, a second ferry service was inaugurated, running from North Sydney, NS, to Argentia, NL.

Nova Scotia to Quebec

Customarily, we don't think of Quebec as a neighbouring province, but the crescent-shaped group of islands in the Gulf of St. Lawrence known as les Îles de la Madeleine (Magdalen Islands) are separated from Nova Scotia by only a

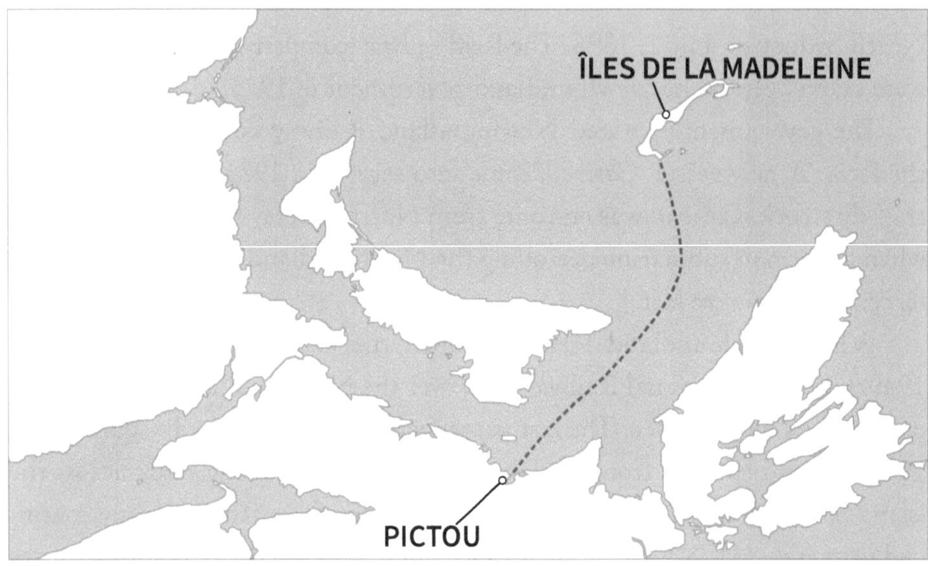

stretch of the Gulf of St. Lawrence. Although the islands are part of Quebec, they are geographically closer to the Maritime provinces. Some of the islands' residents are descendants of Acadians who arrived in 1765 to hunt walruses for a British trader. Many of their fishing boats still proudly fly the Acadian flag.

In spite of the islands' isolated location, the early European inhabitants maintained contact with Nova Scotia. In the mid-nineteenth century, a ferry ran between Pictou and the Magdalen Islands. James Cassidy of Pictou had a contract to carry the mail to the islands, for which he received a subsidy of twenty-five pounds. This had begun as a monthly service, but Cassidy became willing to make two trips per month if he received adequate compensation. Despite the support of many signatories, his request was not granted; presumably, the monthly service continued as before.

Today, a ferry no longer links Nova Scotia to the Magdalen Islands. Visiting Maritimers either fly or take the modern ferry boat departing from Souris on the east coast of Prince Edward Island, arriving at Cap-aux-Meules on Grindstone Island, about a five-hour trip.

International Ferries

Nova Scotia is a relatively short distance from its nearest neighbour in the United States, the state of Maine, separated only by the Gulf of Maine. In the seventeenth century, the French established their colony of Acadie in what is now Nova Scotia. Samuel de Champlain extended his explorations into what is now New England as far south as Cape Cod, and the French maintained an interest in the area which formed a southern extension of Acadie.

For much of the seventeenth century, the French and the English vied for control over the area that began as a collection of colonies in what is now New England. In 1613, Charles de Saint-Étienne de La Tour established a fur trading post at Pentagouet, on the point between the Penobscot and Bagaduce Rivers, on the coast of Maine. The French built a fort at Pentagouet in the 1630s, which changed hands several times until the Treaty of Breda awarded it to the French in 1667. The Dutch were also trying to acquire a foothold in North America, and in 1674 Dutch raiders destroyed the fort.

In 1677, Jean-Vincent d'Abbadie de Saint-Castin built a new settlement higher up the Bagaduce River that became the town of Castine, ME. In the following years, there was frequent communication with the settlement and Port-Royal in Acadie. Despite raids by the English, the area remained under French control until 1713, when it was awarded to the English.

Meanwhile, the town of Boston was expanding to the south. It quickly became the centre of trade in the region. There was frequent communication with the settlements in Acadie that depended on Boston for many imported goods. It also became the administrative centre for New England, its major port, and the base for the English military, until the American Revolution.

Across the water to the north, the population of the French colony of Acadie expanded from Port-Royal to the Minas Basin in the early eighteenth century. Land around the basin and along the rivers was diked and drained, and Acadian communities grew on higher ground overlooking the meadows. These Acadian farming communities were also dependent on trade with Boston. During the Expulsion, the British had Acadians shipped, at least initially, throughout the Thirteen Colonies.

A few years after the Expulsion that occurred between 1755 and 1764, New Englanders took over the vacated farmlands on the Minas Basin. When the former Acadian owners were allowed to return to Nova Scotia, many families were obliged to relocate to the southwestern end of the peninsula. The chief town in the area is Yarmouth, which had been settled by New Englanders in 1761. Land in the surrounding area was granted to the returning Acadians, whose descendants still form the majority of the area's population.

YARMOUTH TO BAR HARBOR AND PORTLAND

Links remained strong between the New England settlers in Yarmouth and the friends and relations they had left behind. Passengers travelled on the merchant ships that brought manufactured goods to Yarmouth from Boston. With so much commercial traffic between the ports, it was some time before the need was felt for a ferry between Yarmouth and New England. When one was initiated, it was in conjunction with Western Counties Railway, later replaced by the Dominion Atlantic Railway that came to Yarmouth in the late 1870s.

The railway brought both freight and passengers destined for Boston and New York to its ferry terminal in Yarmouth. Nova Scotia's tourist industry was beginning to develop, and the Yarmouth Steamship Company was established

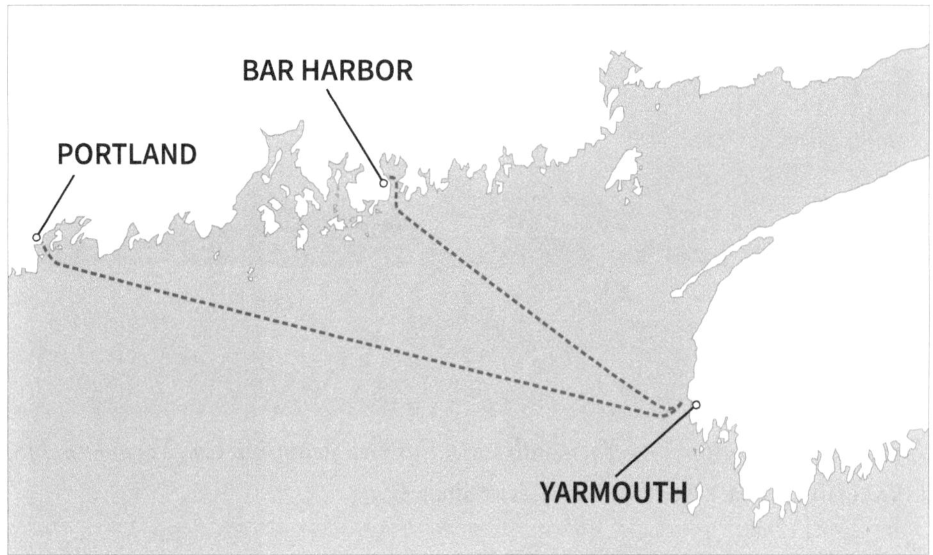

in the 1880s to provide passage to Boston for Nova Scotian travellers and to bring American tourists to Nova Scotia. Over the years since then, several companies have offered a ferry service between the province and ports in New England. They originally carried passengers and freight in conjunction with the railways in both jurisdictions, but more recent ferry services have also carried vehicles.

Steamships have run out of Yarmouth to ports in New England for many years. Merchant vessels carried passengers as well as freight, and Nova Scotian tourists could take a train or coastal ship to Yarmouth, transfer to a ship bound for Portland, ME, or Boston, MA, and travel further from there by rail. With increasing motor traffic after the Second World War, demand grew for a dedicated ferry that would carry vehicles between Nova Scotia and the United States. The shortest distance between Nova Scotia and Maine is between Yarmouth and Bar Harbor, across the Gulf of Maine.

A ferry terminal was built in Yarmouth in 1955, and the following year, Canadian National Railways began to operate a seasonal service with MV *Bluenose*. The CN Marine ferry carried passengers and motor vehicles between the wharf at Yarmouth and ferry terminals in Portland and Bar Harbor. The

Ferries at dock, Boston and Yarmouth Line, Eastern Steamship Co., Yarmouth, NS. [NS ARCHIVES, W. R. MACASKILL 1987-453 NUMBER 3132]

The MV Bluenose, *which travelled from Yarmouth, NS, to Bar Harbor, Maine, from 1982 to 1997.* [NS ARCHIVES]

The CAT *high-speed ferry between Nova Scotia and Maine.* [CO989, PUBLIC DOMAIN, VIA WIKIMEDIA COMMONS]

vehicles drove onto the vessel through hatches in the hull. The ferry was valuable to Nova Scotia businesses wishing to export goods such as lobsters and Christmas trees to New England. It also brought welcome tourists to southwestern Nova Scotia. The service operated daily in summer, and three times a week in winter until the late 1970s, when winter runs were discontinued.

In 1982, the original vessel was replaced by a second MV *Bluenose*, formerly MV *Stena Jutlandica*. Marine Atlantic ran a seasonal operation with this vessel until 1997. Between 1982 and 2004, the *Scotia Prince* sailed from Portland to Yarmouth.

After some delays while a new ferry terminal was constructed at Bar Harbor, the service between Maine and Nova Scotia was re-established with a new ferry, the *CAT*. This high-speed vessel running between Bar Harbor and Yarmouth carries passengers and vehicles from May through October across the Gulf of Maine in just three and a half hours. Over the years, various ferries from Portland have carried travellers and commercial traffic to Yarmouth. The *CAT* resumed operations in 2022 after delays because of mechanical problems, and some controversy over its cost.

Conclusion

Today, Nova Scotian travellers rely on bridges and causeways to cross most bodies of water, and only a handful of ferries are still in use. Travel looked very different in the mid-nineteenth century, when Nova Scotia's many ferries were a major part of the colony's infrastructure.

When you take one of today's ferries—mechanized, efficient, generally reliable, and sometimes free of charge—spare a thought for the men who carried passengers across the same stretch of water in the early to mid-nineteenth century. Originally, men like John Ross and John Pernette rowed heavy boats, often hauling scows that carried horses, wagons, buggies, carriages, or livestock. Called away from their farms or fishing boats, they served the public for a nominal and often inadequate fee and were expected to carry the postman and his horse free of charge. They worked in all weather, enduring the elements to take passengers toward their destinations.

Today's climate change makes it difficult to imagine a time when ferries were seasonal in so many places in Nova Scotia. In winter, ice formed in many of the province's rivers and harbours, making crossing by boat dangerous or impossible. Those boats that continued to run year-round often had to contend with what they called inclement weather to maintain the service, risking damage to their boats and danger to themselves in serving the public.

Most of the ferries that were in operation in the mid-1800s were replaced by either bridges or causeways and made redundant by the end of the century. Those that continued to operate were served by more up-to-date vessels as time went by. The original rowboats and scows gave way in some places to sailboats, followed by steamboats, and then by the diesel-powered vessels that serve as our remaining ferries today.

Neither the ferry operators of the mid-nineteenth century nor their passengers could have foreseen the evolution of today's provincially run ferries, which now operate as part of the highway system. The proposed electric-powered ferries to carry commuters to Halifax from around the Bedford Basin represent the latest example of the changing technology that continues to shape the story of Nova Scotia's ferries.

Acknowledgements

Thanks are due to Judy Campbell and Ray Whitley, who persuaded me to write this book; to the staff of the Nova Scotia Archives, for their help in locating material and dealing with technical problems; to the many anonymous local historians whose websites contain important background information; to editor Paula Sarsen; and to Angela Mombourquette of Nimbus Publishing, for her support and valuable contributions to this project.